Emergence

LIVING LESSONS FROM THE SOIL

STEPHANIE FEGER

Thank You To
Our Book Sponsors!

GRAVES COUNTY
ECONOMIC DEVELOPMENT

Cti Centrifugal Technologies, Inc.
Here when you want us. There when you need us!

STARGAZER
PUBLICATIONS

Emergence: Living Lessons from the Soil

Cover by Madelyn Copperwaite, MC Creative LLC
Editing by Jennifer Crosswhite, Tandem Services Ink
Cover photo taken by Chanel Nicole Co. at Stephanie's favorite florist, Lavender Hill Florals.

First edition, April 2023
ISBN: 978-1-7363872-2-1
Library of Congress Control Number: 2023905166
Created in the United States of America

Learn more about Stephanie Feger at www.StephanieFeger.com. Special discounts are available on quantity book purchases. Contact info@empowerprgroup.com for information.

Contents

Dedication

To those who love to get their hands deep into the dirt, unscathed by the mess it creates and the remnants it leaves under your fingernails; I see you. To those who get weary just thinking about the uncertainty that happens when a seed is planted—in your garden and in your life —and what is needed to help it grow to its fullest potential; I am you. To those who have yet to find their seed of purpose but haven't given up on it one day becoming unearthed. Promise me you won't; I *believe* in you.

This book is dedicated to

… those who are unsure of their future. I understand, for I, too, never know my next step but I've begun to find comfort in uncertainty.

… those who are leery of taking a risk. I understand, for getting outside of that which we are comfortable creates an ambiance that I prefer to steer clear from.

… those who find joy in the mess. I understand you, too, for it's been in my single steps with no apparent purpose that I've come to find peace in the chaos.

Life isn't about knowing; it's about trusting. It's not about loving where you are; it's about being willing to change when called to. There's more to be done—deep down in the dirt found within—and getting dirt under your nails is a necessity for growth.

To those of you who are ready to emerge, here's to cultivating the conditions to make it happen.

The Teacher Beneath Our Feet

Living and *really* living are distinct, much like hearing versus listening.

While both require breaths that fill you, motions to move you and thoughts to shape you, there is a subtle but life-changing difference that could be overlooked if you don't intentionally take notice. Some see the difference as minuscule, while others mock it. I likely would as well, if not for my garden's revelations, the lessons I've unearthed with my hands deep in the soil.

SOME CALL IT PURPOSE. OTHERS REFER TO IT AS INTENTIONALITY.

Mindfulness and mindset are a typical match made in heaven. I wrap it up with a handmade bow called awareness. This type of conscious living is found when your breaths become purposeful, your motions become meaningful, and your thoughts become directional.

When you really live, you no longer let your unconscious guide you. You take the reins when possible to steer purposeful action. When a challenge happens—and it will—you trust all things work together for good.

It's easy to become engulfed in daily minutia, and frequently I question if that's society's endgame. What would happen if we spent less time trying to keep up with the Joneses? Here's a hint. We'd buy less, disconnect more and rediscover what living is. That goes against the goals of our culture, but it's at the heart of why we are here and what we are called to do.

Don't let me fool you. I constantly have to pull myself out of the swirling plague of comparisons, imposter syndrome and their evil stepsister, perfectionism. It's effortless to fall into life's motions where responsibility guides steps and you become one of many fish in a school led by someone else entirely. While accountability is important, if it's the sole driving force, then I'll be moving through my days because that's what I'm supposed to do, not because it's what I dream of. And in the process, I may not be living the life I'm called to live.

This type of conscious living is easy to adopt and hard to alter.

When I find myself letting life happen instead of making it, I retreat to my backyard where I can get my hands dirty and soul replenished. It may sound counterintuitive—dirt and cleanliness together—but it's when I'm working with the land, I intentionally awaken to notice that growth is coming and always happening.

I go to the one place where words aren't required to be spoken.
I go where listening is the most essential of skills.
I go where my heart feels most alive, and my soul is fertilized.
I go to my garden.

Most weekends of my childhood, my dad and I would each pack a small overnight bag and trek to my grandparents' farm a few hours from our house to work. I didn't have a job there—not in the sense of what a job means to most. Instead, my job was to just be, and just being took unique shapes each weekend. Whether I was wading in the shallow creek bed or daydreaming in the treehouse my dad had made, my job description was always totally attainable: to be intentionally quiet, to be consciously present and to actively listen.

Of all the spots I wandered to on the farm, my favorite place to accomplish my weekend recharge was in the garden.

My grandparents' sweet garden was where I learned the importance of sweat equity and boy did everyone invest their fair share in that small slice of dirt. We tilled. We dug. We planted. We fertilized. We loved. We prayed. We shared. And the best part was when my grandma would collect lettuce, cucumbers, onions and tomatoes to make a delicious vinegar tomato and cucumber salad with a side of wilted lettuce. It was there she was living, breathing proof that we are the fruits of our labor. We ate together, always, and when we did, I could taste her love.

I was *really* living.

That feeling can be captivating, and if there's anything worth being drawn to like a mosquito to a zapper, conscious living is a wise choice (and a much safer option).

Planted deep in my formative years, a love for gardening firmly took root. So much so that when my husband and I purchased our first home, a large enough yard for a plentiful vegetable garden was a nonnegotiable. We wanted three bedrooms—one for the two of us and one for each of the two kids we had hoped to one day have (only to find out later we would have three, and those bedrooms would become shared spaces). We hoped for a quiet neighborhood—one where we could take long walks and wave at neighbors. Honestly, though, I cared less about what was inside the house and more about the outside potential.

I inherited my earthy brunette locks and spit-fire temperament from relatives, but I'm most proud of the green thumb handed down through generations on both sides of my family tree. Learning side-by-side with my dad and his mom tending our family's vegetable garden to cherishing moments with my mom and her mom while gaining skills to nurture African violets and Christmas cactuses made it clear that growing is baked in my DNA. (And if you doubt your ability to keep a plant alive, rest assured it's a skill within reach, I promise.)

Many life learnings took place in my little slice of heaven nestled in the backyard of our first family home. Early morning visits to the garden offered hope with the day's fresh dew. Late afternoon waterings replenished both my plants and my soul. Years of laying manure on the garden between planting seasons offered an annual reminder to fertilize ourselves, especially during the dark and downtrodden times. And the life I've met along the way—from harmless spiders spinning artistic webs to unexpected but often welcomed bunny nests —proved that there is room for everyone when I'm consciously living and consciously loving.

Those teachable moments embedded in me like a splinter I welcomed, not one I wanted to extract. They weren't always easy to digest, but each contributed to my growth.

Years later, our home was maxed out of space for all the stuffed animals, educational toys and clothing for every season, so we knew it was time. Our home had given us all it could, and it was time to let another family absorb its living lessons. Moving was imperative to our continued growth... physically, for our now family of five had outgrown our current space, and personally, for more learning begged for discovery.

The X on our house hunting treasure map was an expansive space to welcome a substantial garden, a fruit-bearing orchard and endless personal, emotional and spiritual growth. The day we set foot on the twenty-five-acre farm that would soon become ours, we got a glimpse of what heaven might be like on earth. I can testify that this place we call home has witnessed immense growth, both in our garden and within each of us.

THE SOIL HAS BECOME MY LIFELONG TEACHER.

It mentors me when I hide between my tomato plants, plucking weeds that have the persistence to find a crack in our recycled newspaper barrier and attempt to derail our gardening plans. While plucking their invasive hopes, I also weed the negativity running rampant within. The soil speaks louder when I watch squash vines weaving through chicken wire, determined to not let anything hinder its growth. If plants can be inventive in growth, the soil tells me, you can too. My garden is among a handful of places where I can feel God in my midst as the wind hugs each plant purposefully, just as He does me.

It may be quiet in the garden, but it's where God speaks the most.
It may be slow in the garden, but it's where growth is not rushed.
It may be muddy in the garden, but it's where I feel most clean and seen.

So much learning happens here, tilling through challenges and accepting them as nourishment for life's season. I find rest in the mess, a place most seek to avoid, and I also find purpose. Grateful to my family for instilling a love for the land, I'm living proof that not all seeds come in small packets and are immersed deep in the earth. Many times, they are found in people and passed on to others. You may enjoy a bountiful harvest when planting a vegetable garden, but you will reap more than any picking basket can hold when you sow seeds of compassion, hope and love to all you meet.

Just like a well-tended garden, our lives can yield an abundant harvest, one that is poised to pollinate others, leaving all completely and utterly filled.

PART ONE

The Seed

It all starts with a seed.

A thought.
A dream.
A plan.
A passion.
A life.

While your calling wasn't written on your birth certificate, you were born with a purpose meant to guide your life's path. You have seeds within you—likely several—that, when the conditions are right, can take root and help you bloom into who you are destined to be.

The question isn't if a seed exists, but if you've discovered it yet. Unearthing your purpose isn't always easy to do, but like a seed, it starts somewhere purposeful and many times starts small.

The Lesson

~~~

As I stretched my neck from side to side, it cracked just like that of the textbook's spine I was holding that morning. The book was still stiff from its newness, and I, too, was stiff from the new position I unexpectedly assumed. The front page of the textbook that proudly bore the word *Life*[1] in bold print served a reminder that what I was doing went beyond simply teaching my children life science. I had an opportunity to change their lives in the process.

I once dreamed of being a teacher.
But I never expected it to emerge this way.

In elementary school, I would pretend to be a teacher with two other Stephanies during after-school care. We bonded over a shared name and shared interests. I always begged to be the English teacher, go figure. In high school, I pondered what a full-time educator could be like as I watched my history teacher jump from tabletop to tabletop, anything to pull us into the magical world of the past. It wasn't until college, however, that I seriously considered becoming an educator. I even almost dabbled into it as my major, until I made a pact with myself.

The collegiate level is calling.
Get a degree. Get some experience.
Then get a doctorate and teach at a university.

That was my plan, until I had kids. Then I understood that, for me, being an educator was an everyday job, not a nine-to-five. At least not until the pandemic hit.

The world was in complete chaos, mine included. Like the rest of the population, we rushed to the store to snatch up as much toilet paper as allowed along with non-perishable items. My hands trembled as I stood in line outside of Sam's Club with a mask hiding my identity and thankfully my fear, awaiting a turn for a real-life game of *Supermarket Sweep*. My mind swirled with unknowns, and the only thing that I knew for certain was I needed to prioritize my kids.

How could I create a stable environment for them when life was anything but? How could I pour goodness into them when the news was doing the opposite? How could I be what they desperately needed when I wasn't sure what I needed?

Homeschooling was a new consideration for our family, even before the pandemic descended like a heavy fog. My husband, Cory, and I brainstormed what it would take for us to educate our littles. We toured enrichment programs, visited hybrid homeschool facilities and learned what a homeschool co-op was. This path was one we were already heading down, but the pandemic gave us an extra nudge towards it.

READY OR NOT, I ADDED A NEW HAT TO MY COLLECTION OF MANY.

Next to wife, mom, entrepreneur, author and friend was now teacher. I was filled with trepidation but equally invigorated. This new adventure would be amazing for all, I was determined. While others frantically scoured the internet for toilet paper, which was in major deficit, I happily searched for the perfect homeschooling curriculum, which became my new favorite pastime.

When our textbooks arrived, I was like a kid in a candy shop, except the rush came from smelling the new pages of knowledge that awaited instead of ingesting more sugar than anyone should at once. Upon a quick glance, the math lesson plans appeared doable, which was a worry of mine since I hadn't dabbled in it for years. The history materials intrigued me as I could discover and rediscover alongside my kids. But my favorite was our family life science curriculum.

Broken into three parts—the world of plants, animals and the human body—the book was overflowing with opportunity. In addition to the learnings found on each page, I was most excited about our family learning about life together, in unison... no masks required. It was just us, working as a unit.

Whatever mayhem occurred outside of our walls didn't matter when our homeschool class was in session. It was just what the mind, body and soul needed and longed for most.

Each morning, after munching on breakfast while watching a cartoon, my three kids (in kindergarten, first grade and third grade at the time) and I would meander to the hidden gem above our garage. This room housed my blooming business, and it was also where our learning occurred. Our classroom was cozy, complete with a plush rug where we would all congregate together for the daily science lesson.

There, while the kids rolled around on the floor, we learned what life meant, literally, and that there are more living things than just us humans. Later in the curriculum we explored all parts of the magnificent human body and the zoo of animals we had accumulated thus far. But the start of the year kicked off with plant science, and I was in heaven.

We explored kingdoms and classifications and gained insights on the types of trees and flowering plants before we got to the section on seeds.

For little minds, sometimes you have to go big before you go small, zoom out before you can focus in. How can you ask questions if your mind isn't ready? You wouldn't be concerned how flowers come to be if you weren't aware of the flower in the first place.

Each chapter offered an experiment to augment learning. Sometimes we glazed past, deciding as a group if it was something worthy of executing. But when the seed dissection experiment was mentioned, it became a requirement by this teacher. I meticulously followed each step because, to my surprise, I had never explored what laid beneath a seed's protective casing. I had dissected frogs and pig hearts, but never a seed. I was ready.

I gathered a handful of seeds from the pantry (which were actually beans we had planned to eat later) and soaked them in warm water the night prior. We collectively made our way to the kitchen counter for lunch and to where our experiment awaited. Our first observation was that the warm water had loosened the seed's coating which is what was holding it all together, keeping the seed safe until the conditions were right for it to break free.

Huddled together, three brunettes and a blondie, we observed the tiny bean's hilum, which is a small scar on the outside of the seed where the seed was attached to its flower once. A belly button of sorts, we concluded. Slowly, we peeled back its coating to reveal what lay underneath. A small white differentiation was visible, and our book confirmed it was its radicle. What a radical concept, I thought, that this small seed had the beginnings of roots from the start. Connected to the end was a small white leaf, the plumule it's called, which we discovered would have been the first leaf the plant ever had.

THERE, IN A TINY SEED, WAS THE BEGINNINGS OF LIFE.

Stashed away in our pantry, dormant for years, that bean was jammed packed with potential. Its exterior left much to be desired, but beneath its surface was the makings of something downright breathtaking. Life. That single bean held the potential to create life too. How many more beans could have stemmed from this one? Countless, I'm sure.

We closed our textbooks, ready to devour a lunch of deli meat, string cheese and fresh fruit, and I connected the very meaningful dots this message offered. "This bean had been with us for years, but no plant had sprouted from it," I recalled. They agreed, because if it had our pantry would be overrun with a plant problem. "But within it is potential. What would it have needed to thrive?" I asked. Each of my three kids offered an answer from their learnings.

"Water," one said.
"Air," another offered up.
"Sun," the final tossed out.
"And a warm home... some soil possibly," I wrapped up the lesson stating.

Until the conditions were right, nothing would happen with this seed. It would remain a quiet resident among others in its familiar bag. But silence doesn't diminish potential. A lack of growth doesn't indicate a lack of possibility.

Everything a seed needs is found within it. All it's looking for is the support to break free from its cover and the conditions to help it thrive.

As I watched my children devour their meal, I realized that we all have seeds within us waiting to be discovered. Sometimes we are the ones uncovering those seeds, and other times, we are the ones planting them in the lives of those around us. Sometimes we need to give our seeds a warm bath to gently awaken them, and other times, we are all the warmth needed for others to activate theirs.

So much life is around us and within us, and everything our seeds need to thrive is packaged within, awaiting its opportunity to break free and blossom.

---

1. God's Design® Life, MasterBooks Curriculum by Debbie and Richard Lawrence, Fourth Edition: January 2016

The Packet

As a little girl, I would incessantly bombard my parents with endless questions about any and everything I could possibly dream of seeking knowledge about. I would happily trade outdoor sports for quiet reading time. Learning was my favorite thing to pursue.

Why is the sky blue?
What color would you rather it be, they'd ask in response.

Where did babies come from?
You don't want to know, was their frequent answer.

Can I have a sibling?
That question never worked since I remained an only child.

Why do I have to do what you tell me to?
Because, and that was the final answer.

Every kid usually asks some variation of these in their formative years. My grandma soothed my exhausted parents' annoyances by asking a question in return when they would grumble about my endless inquiries.

"How is she supposed to learn if she doesn't ask?" (I'm sure my parents wanted to answer her rhetorical question with inappropriate word choices but knew better. As a mother now, I know I would!)

Instead, my mom would savor a deep breath, realizing without answers will only come more questions, and answer each as best she could. My dad, on the other hand, crafted a creative response that left him dodging any future questions. "I don't know that answer," he would boldly proclaim. "Remember, I'm not a teacher." At that time, I believed that teachers must be the most knowledgeable of all, so this gave him a hall pass. Lucky duck!

One of the questions that puzzled me most was each time we merged onto a highway. Others see the cracked pavement as a mere means to get from point A to point B. But not me. I always questioned where the road began. Was our car the first one on it, or was there always someone in front of us? Did the highway start at one beach and end at another on the opposite side of the continent?

I asked these questions before ever sitting behind the wheel with freedom right in front of me. Later, I discovered that some roads have beginnings and endings much closer to home than originally seemed. Some do end on a sandy beach and others continue past where they should, over vast waters to connect us to other beautiful treasures. (Those roads, the ones that are built in Florida connecting islands to the mainland, terrify me!)

It was then that I considered maybe it didn't matter where the beginning was, but rather where the beginning could take us. We will likely never know if we are the first on the road, but we are the first on our road. And as the driver of our own lives, with our hands gripped to our steering wheels, we can determine what we do with our beginnings... with our seeds.

EACH SPRING I FIND MYSELF GETTING THE ITCH.

No, not the literal one I do end up getting after hours outdoors spending time fulfilling my figurative one. I'm talking about the feeling I get when I begin to feel the cold tinge in the air each morning lightening up and the pollen begins to crowd in the wind giving many people the sneezes. I can barely wait when I see the dormant trees begin to awaken as blooms remind us that there is indeed life after winter. That's when I get the itch to start planting.

While I'm no Farmer's Almanac follower, I do subscribe to the local "tried and true" for planting. Here in Kentucky, everything in horse-country is determined by the Derby season, even vegetable garden planting.

In fact, the rule of thumb in my neck of the woods is to plant your garden on or near Derby, which is the first Saturday in May. No sooner for fear of frost and not much later or your crop beginnings won't survive the summer's heat. At least that's what they say, and while I don't know who they are, I always follow their advice. That year was no exception.

The sun was giving my shoulders a heat massage as I knelt to get as close to the soil as possible. Later, muscles in my body I didn't even know existed would ache, making it hard to maneuver as easily as I could that very moment. But it was worth it then as it always is, for that day I was beginning my garden's annual planting. And what better seed to welcome in than the radish.

RADISHES. WHO LIKES THEM? REALLY?

While I have found various recipes to use this root vegetable, it will never be my favorite to harvest. Each year I plant them, and each year I end up with several handfuls of burgundy bitterness, unsure what other foods complement them best. Just before they ripen beyond recovery, I usually resort to pulling out a salt shaker and eating them raw.

What I do with the vegetable is obsolete. It doesn't deflect from the joy it brings me as I hear the quick rip opening the seed packet.

A packet of possibilities.
Endless. Unknowing. Patiently awaiting.
So small yet full of so much potential.

As I gently tore open the seed packet, I looked closely at the tiny opportunity of life held in my palm. Each seed was as unique as the next. To the naked eye, each seed looked similar to the next—a small clump of soil could be a distant cousin of the radish seed—but upon close inspection, each was nuanced and individualized.

As with everything in life, growth all starts with action. The radish seeds could remain in the seed packet hidden in the depths of my garage for years without any change.

They were patient and would have waited if I made them. And since they had no legs of their own, they knew they needed help to get where they needed to go. Luckily for them, they didn't have to find their end destination after traveling the digestive tract of an animal, which is a typical dissemination technique nature relies on. All they needed were my hands and my willingness to act.

Those seeds were only useful to me when they germinated, offering up a not-so-tasty radish in return. But to give them an opportunity required movement on my part. I had to rip open the packet and pour the countless seeds into my palm (as well as the picking up of all the ones that I spilled too, which is nearly impossible). And then, after the soil was parted, I had to welcome them to their forever home.

After I dug a small trench into the garden's soil, I methodically trickled the seeds into the land hoping that they would fulfill their end of the bargain. My action required another action, and something magical began to happen the moment they were planted. Not more than an inch or so under the topsoil, the seed enjoyed a stretch from its hibernation and got to work, later offering us a radish for our mixed greens salad in return.

Not a moment before it was sowed—or countless other vegetable varieties that have called my garden home—could it begin to fulfill its purpose.

The only way it reaches its fullest potential was if we did it together. It required fertile soil, full of the nutrients it needed to succeed. The rain showers mixed with the summer's warmth were required to continue feeding its ego. Then it could create the vegetable that only amazing chefs can disguise in their cuisine. Only then, could it be picked and enjoyed, its purpose completed.

Every year, as I welcome seeds into our vegetable garden, I sit in anticipation knowing something amazing is bound to happen the moment the seed is covered, unexposed to the naked eye but magical nonetheless. No matter the seed and no matter the variety, I remain equally energized knowing the packet is one full of possibilities and to be at the start of seeing that—to be the person that makes that happen —is downright empowering.

Rest assured I am keenly aware that we are talking about merely a folded over envelope with a handful of tiny seeds most people overlook. In fact, they do so daily when walking among a poorly cared for front yard that's beaming in pride of its dandelions. You may turn up your nose at the carelessness of the yard's owner, but a child sees it as their playground, complete with fuzzy flowers begging for a child's forceful exhale to distribute the invasive plant's lifeline.

You and I know that those seeds create weeds, and my vegetable seeds create meals, but the joy is all the same.

THE ITCH TO PLANT DOESN'T ONLY STIR UP WHEN SPRINGTIME ALLERGIES ARE IN FULL SWING.

Since the conditions for seed growth varies, not all seeds require a perfect pH balance to germinate. In fact, some don't need a vegetable garden at all. These seeds live within us and require the same delicate care as I offer my radish seeds. They will remain dormant if you let them. Only you can create the conditions of positive support, nurturing influences and purposeful action to ensure they are methodically planted and constantly watered. You are the action they need to thrive.

Finding these seeds, however, can prove challenging if you don't intentionally pull out a metal detector and seek out your own self-worth. I unearth my seeds in one of three places—during a relaxing evening soak, while driving my kids to and from their commitments or deep in the night when I am lost in my dreams. I suppose it's then that my soil is the most fertile, and my willingness to discover the tiny seeds is most prevalent. I've found the seeds of fresh career paths, innovative solutions to current challenges and new life changes—all buried within, begging to be planted in soil to take root.

Like radish seed packets, your seeds come with directions, but instead of reading them, you must feel them. Your seed's directions won't tell you how deep to plant or whether they prefer direct sunlight or not. They won't dictate the time of your life that you should plant it like the radish packet will.

Your seed packet leaves a lot for you to figure out, which can be frustrating. However, it's part of the process to help you prepare and fertilize your soil.

Our seeds tell a story—our story—if we take action from them. You get to choose when you are ready, how your soil is prepared and what energy you offer them. You are your seed packet, and you know what your seeds need to thrive. Your seeds of possibilities are always ready and always waiting.

All they need is an action to be taken to get them planted.
All they need is the possibility for a beginning.
All they need is you.

The Cave

~~~

While it may appear differently, I don't do most things on purpose. If I hurt feelings, it's never intentional. My timing, even when it's impeccable, is usually by happenstance. My words aren't always calculated, and my actions often stem from impulsive gut instincts. And many inspired moments often occur in the most unexpected of places.

When I noticed a seed I had planted on the verge of blooming, I realized that what I do unintentionally may still happen deliberately at just the right moment when someone is completely open to hearing the message. It may not have been with a particular goal in mind, but it is still, nonetheless, planting something meaningful in the heart of someone who needs it most.

MY DAD ENJOYS IMPROMPTU DAY TRIPS WITH MY KIDS, TAKING THEM ON "P-PAW ADVENTURES."

During summer breaks, he would plan getaways with my kids, creating lasting memories with the three people he loved most. That year, my oldest two, Eli and Lyndi, looked forward to their weekly outings while my youngest, Luke, was still too tiny for these explorations. They would visit museums and parks, jump on trampolines for hours upon end and paint pottery together, all of which became core memories for my dad and my kids. But it was the trip to the cave that stood out most.

THE NIGHT BEFORE THE ADVENTURE, MY DAD SHARED THAT HE WANTED TO TAKE THEM TO MARENGO CAVE, A LIMESTONE CAVE SYSTEM IN SOUTHERN INDIANA.

Living close to Mammoth Cave, one of the world's longest known cave systems living under the soil of part of Kentucky, one would think we would frequent the home of bats. (Instead, we savor the fact that Louisville is the home of the Slugger Bats.)

Raising kids was hard enough though, and trying to safely herd them in the depths of cave darkness wasn't on my agenda.

My dad had taken Eli to a cave before, but I kept the experience a surprise for Lyndi and eagerly anticipated hearing her thoughts afterward.

When my crew pulled into the paved drive in my dad's pickup truck that evening, it was apparent they had an unforgettable day. Eli couldn't outtalk the pace of his thoughts as they stumbled over each while he tried to share the stories behind the handfuls of copper pennies he pulled out of his pockets. While deep in the cave, he found a coin trail, not knowing they were coins others threw up on the ceilings trying to get them to stick for good luck. The ones he collected were fallen wishes but full of luck, as he saw them.

Lyndi was thrilled with the mermaid backpack my dad bought her at the gift shop after their tour. She loved anything that indulged her hoarding tendency in secret, and this backpack would do the trick.

After the sun had set and each kid was freshly bathed, I cuddled with Lyndi on her bed to relive the experience of the day through her eyes.

Was she scared of going deep into the earth?
Was it exhilarating hearing the echoes all around?
Did the darkness worry her?
Or did she enjoy the adventure into the unknown?

Her gentle voice whispered stories about her favorites from the day, the stalactites and the stalagmites, although at her young age, she had much more creative names for each. She nervously glanced around the room while sharing how she accidentally touched one when no one was looking. The claustrophobic space didn't faze her, and when I asked her how she felt when they turned off all the lights—a moment that made me queasy—she imparted a piece of life advice that one would expect a parent to share, not a child. She summed up how she handled the feeling of complete fear deep in a cave with a moment of complete and utter darkness.

"I was brave."

I HAVE TO BELIEVE THAT I'M NOT THE ONLY ONE WHO THINKS IN SONG.

When someone asks a question, usually my answer pops up in a lyric from a song that's been on repeat like a broken record in my head. When my kids were younger and Eli would ask me what time it was, I would immediately respond, "It's time for lunch"—whether it was or not—and hum the tune of a Bubble Guppies song. While gazing at my daughter, wondering how I got so lucky to be her mom, I couldn't help but sing Van Morrison's "Brown Eyed Girl."

When I was stressed, concerned if I had capacity to complete a project, I would answer my own worries with my favorite lyrics from a Troll's song: "I really hope I can do it. Because they're all depending on me." With the tune of "Get Back Up Again," it always reminded me that no matter what, I could get back up!

Some songs became meaningful responses to questions that occurred in daily life. Others, however, became full, blown out anthems. They became lyrics to live by and ones I belted when I was alone in a completely quiet car—or when the car was so chaotic I needed a reminder of why I was doing exactly what I was doing. Songs hold deep meaning for me, but only a select few have truly become my anthems.

I hadn't seen her live in concert, but I felt a deep connection with her music, almost like I knew her personally. While I didn't have every song of hers committed to memory, one I knew inside and out, from the pitch to the melody and every single riff. Sara Barielles's song, "Brave," is my spirit song. I recited it daily, like a meditation enthusiast would a chant. And without knowing, it had given me purpose, and it gave Lyndi purpose too.

If you haven't heard it yet, take four minutes to watch the music video. Soak up each lyric as a reminder that you have the power to be amazing, your words can be used for good, you can always try something new, and different isn't something to avoid, it's something to embrace. And when it comes down to it, all you really need to tackle the day head on is the courage to be brave.

Bravery. My daughter had it without my knowing, likely from hearing me belt out the song hundreds of times without a care in the world and from seeing me push through challenges despite my fears.

She knew every lyric to the song, and her eyes would light up when I played it on my phone for us. In fact, she would often request "our favorite song," and without her having to say anything more, I knew exactly which one she meant.

Bravery wasn't an attribute my daughter needed to hoard in her new mermaid backpack. She unknowingly offered me a seed in return for the one I had planted in her. On a day when I was feeling anything but brave, I needed to find more fight, and helplessness wasn't an option.

I had been navigating worrisome health issues for months and had reached a point of wanting to give up. But a recent doctor's appointment had charged me to persevere, with more tests to run and answers to be uncovered. I had found myself like my daughter had, in a dark cave with the lights turned off, but it was time to pull out my life's anthem, choose bravery and find my way back to the light.

If my daughter could be brave, so could I.

WHAT WAS BRAVERY ANYWAY?

I pondered that thought, questioning if it meant accepting my fate or uncovering my destiny. Walking the tightrope with doom looming, sitting in a box of snakes or diving in a pond with crocodiles? While these actions can exhibit bravery, Lyndi was living proof that being brave didn't require such extremes.

Instead, bravery is standing up for what you believe in, even if it is opposing the popular opinion.

It's being you in a sea of people who may not understand you and planting seeds anyway.

It's smiling in the face of challenge, for you know that storms strengthen your stem.

It's taking a deep breath while having the courage to continue your walk down the path of the unknown.

It's believing something bigger is to come and knowing despite the outcome of lingering tests, all will be well.

Being brave doesn't mean you accept your situation. Instead, it means that you accept the *you* in your situation. You accept that you have the power to control only you, and despite the struggles to want to give up, you choose not to.

It's beautiful how someone so small has the power to do something so big. A seed's gift isn't equivalent to its size and doesn't define its worth. At the ripe age of five, Lyndi's authentic smile and simple word choice reminded me that the only way for a seed to grow is for it to bravely accept the darkness, the pressures coming at it from all sides, and push forward anyway. The light isn't far outside of reach. In fact, someone may have their hand on the switch ready to invite you back into it.

No matter what life path you are on, remember that if a tiny seed and a tiny person can be brave, you have the power to as well.

The Pests

W hen my husband and I took the leap to buy a farm, the endless land excited me, just asking for my special gardening touch. I daydreamed where the gazebo laced with fragrant wisteria would overlook the fishing pond. I saw acres of soybeans, providing an endless supply of edamame for my edamame-loving family. I knew precisely where the raspberry bushes and grapevines would bear the most delicious fruit for this soon-to-be winemaker and where the pumpkin patch would roll over the hill visible from our porch.

I ENVISIONED SO MUCH, HOWEVER THAT VISION NEARLY DISSIPATED THE FIRST DAY I PLANTED MY GARDEN.

We were in the middle of building a house, so building a garden—albeit an important part of my soul's needs—was an afterthought. We lacked capacity to manage the acreage before living full-time on the farm, so we earmarked a handful of acres for us to tinker with and allowed a neighbor to bail hay on the rest. A smart move, I thought, until the garden I envisioned was supposed to be on the land I had just promised to a neighbor. I had to think quickly if I wanted any hopes for fresh, homegrown goodness.

It was late spring, prime time for planting season in Kentucky. We got in touch with the son of a local farmer who tilled gardens as a side hustle, and after showing him our spaces for consideration, he found the perfect spot not far from the house on a slight rolling hill. With enthusiasm brimming over, he tilled up a plot larger than any garden I had ever imagined.

As planting day arrived, my heart raced with excitement as my hands dug into the newly fertile topsoil. Little did I know that while I dug in, something else dug back.

My youngest, Luke, has always loved gardening, so he and I trekked through the mess of new construction to our soon-to-be vegetable sanctuary. Several boxes accompanied us, jam packed with a variety of tomato and green pepper starters. Since our gardening tools had been packed in storage for our big move, we each held a plastic garden spade that the Easter Bunny had so timely gifted the kids that year. (Don't judge! Parents have to work with what they've got.)

Luke used his Paw Patrol-themed spade to sever the dirt mounds formed by the excavators digging our basement, a more captivating experience than planting for him. I used the Batman spade to dig much smaller holes meant for my vegetable "babies." Each seed and plant starter I strategically placed in the soil was a baby I felt called to protect. Covered in cayenne pepper as a deterrent for the deer and raccoons, each plant was nurtured and loved, knowing one day its fruit would nourish my loved ones.

We worked hard that day, Luke and me. With unwavering dedication, he dug in the dirt until every inch of him was caked with it, from his tousled blonde mane to the soles of his new shoes. My hard work, on the other hand, was evident in my clothes drenched in sweat, proof of my labored effort. After six hours of planting, only half of the garden was placed.

A slow and steady pace was necessary, I told myself. Nothing can rush planting.

THE DRIVE TO THE HOUSE WE WERE STAYING AT WHILE WE WERE BUILDING OUR FUTURE HOME WAS A REFRESHING "WINDOW-DOWN" JOURNEY.

The fresh air both helped soak up my sweat and omit its stench. While enjoying the wind in my hair, I ran my fingers through it and down to the base of my neck, and when I did, I was in for an unpleasant surprise.

An unwelcome clump of dirt perched at my neck's base, which I scratched off, hoping to save time in the shower later. As the caked-on dirt dislodged from my neck and tumbled into my palm I brought it down to inspect before tossing it on the floor. The dirt no longer was problematic; what was actively moving on it was.

A tick.

The blood-sucking pest had decided to take a vacation from its perfectly humble abode and take residence on my skin, burying deep into my hairline. Its body intact, staring at me as if it was preparing its next move, I freaked, I fumbled and I nervously tossed the micro-scopic nuisance toward the ground, although it landed on my blue jeans. Before I could flick it off, the rational side of my brain opted to toss it out the window instead so it couldn't find its way back to me. Brave Stephanie picked it up and let the wind lead it to its demise.

I was traumatized. I loved farm living and the freedom it provided. I savored the echoes found in the wind, the smells of wildflowers and the sights of an endless sea of green. I loved every ounce of its being, except for the ticks. I could handle carpenter bees and even mosquitos. I'd deal with the horseflies and the worms, I told myself. But for the love of everything, I wasn't sure I could deal with ticks.

To sweeten the deal, later that evening I found one of the tick's relatives on the bottom portion of my shirt when I pulled it up to wipe sweat from my brow. Two. In one day. I considered putting up a For Sale sign and moving downtown where ticks would be traded in for pollution. But over the entourage of worried thoughts was the beckoning of my garden. Only half of my babies were tucked into their soil homes. The rest waited for me, and I knew, as with any seed, their potential wasn't possible until I took action and planted them.

> They depended on me, and while it sounded like the ideal time to start waving the white flag of surrender, I was needed. Seeds and vegetable plant starters needed planting. I had work to do.

It took me a week to muster up the courage to go back to the garden, and when I did, I walked cautiously while making a truce with the ticks. *I didn't kill your kin, so please don't eat me.* Covered in bug spray (four layers at least), I dug the first hole for my weary tomato plants. While initially hesitant to kneel in the dirt, something unexpectedly dawned on me.

It was time to accept them. The ticks, that is.

No matter how much I despised their existence, they would never leave. I couldn't have a talk with their leader and make a deal for their departure. They were there for the long haul, and so was I. I had to accept them, and in turn, I had to come to understand them.

My mind found new clarity, and my tense muscles began to relax as I sunk down into the soil. Upon closer look, the ticks weren't the only creepy-crawling critters surrounding me. Earthworms wiggled free from the compressed soil I had loosened, and bees danced within earshot. Here in my earthly heaven were a multitude of pests just doing their jobs alongside me doing mine. I had to accept that I shared a space, purposefully, with an arch nemesis.

I found peace with the ticks and the rest of the insects I despised. I didn't love them, don't get me wrong. But I learned to tolerate them nonetheless. Together, our efforts were in alignment. I needed their work to loosen the soil, helping my seeds grow roots. The bees were pivotal to plant pollination, helping them to grow to their fullest potential. As for the ticks, I still don't understand their purpose, but they must have one other than latching on to me. Whatever reason that is must be something that validates their existence.

WHEN YOU ARE READY TO PLANT YOUR SEEDS, YOU MUST ACKNOWLEDGE THAT YOUR SURROUNDINGS MAY NOT APPEAR PERFECT.

Your soil may contain squirmy worms and blood-sucking pests, and you may want to pack everything up and torch it. But you have a choice: *You can let the nuisances and challenges defeat you or you can learn to accept them.* The path you choose will determine your seed's destiny.

That day, all I wanted was a planted garden. I was tired physically, and sick and tired emotionally from the bugs. "Why couldn't it all be easy?" I said on repeat, and the answer to my own question was simple.

It was sweat equity, and nothing in life is ever as simple as it seems.

Gardening isn't a fast-food joint. It isn't an on-demand experience, and it doesn't come with free shipping. It demands dedicated work, manual labor and open-ended trust and, in return, it promises to zap your energy and push you to relinquish control, confident the seeds will fulfill their end of the bargain. Accept that the pests that show up —whether they are your negative thoughts, the naysayers you encounter or the bloodsuckers that fight you—are meant to loosen your soil, providing you and your seeds with the nutrients needed most.

Different seeds require different conditions for growth, but all require trust. Trust the process, knowing God will provide exactly what you and your seed need. Relinquish control and worry, embrace the imperfections and even the pests, and trust that together, all will grow and flourish.

The One

Like most Sundays, Cory and I packed up my laptop and three-inch binder filled with teacher manuals to guide that week's Sunday school discussion. For several years we spent an hour each week with a dozen or so second graders to help prepare them for their First Communion, a meaningful sacrament in the Catholic faith.

With the exciting sacrament just weeks away, and since we had nearly concluded our preparation discussion, we pivoted our weekly message from the sacrament itself to what the sacrament called us to do afterward.

Prior to any deep dive discussion, our curriculum offered a brief cartoon that aligned with the weekly message. Over the weeks together, the class had watched so many of these videos that they could hum the tune of the opening ditty the moment it began. Even though the videos were a bit silly at times, the kids enjoyed them, and I appreciated the change of pace they offered.

THE MESSAGE THAT SUNDAY WAS OF A STORY OUTLINING A STARFISH AND A YOUNG BOY.

He was taking a walk on a beach when he found countless starfish on the shore. In awe of their beauty he paused to soak in the experience. While doing so, he realized that while the sand was their home, without water, they would soon perish. He had a mission, and he was determined to help each make their way home.

An elderly man walked by, taking notice of this young boy's persistence. With purpose, he would pick up a starfish and, with all his might, throw it as far into the ocean's depths as his strength allowed. The boy didn't appear fazed by the vast amount of starfish, but the elderly man did and brought it to the boy's attention that it wasn't feasible to help them all.

"You'll never be able to rescue each" he acknowledged.
"You may be right," the boy replied. "But at least I can help this one."

I opened discussion on the topic with the class, asking if they would have done what the boy was attempting to do, despite knowing that they may not be able to help all the starfish.

Eagerly, the class shouted in unison that of course they would; they would help as many as possible. While I appreciated their answer, I questioned its accuracy, for I knew how easy it was to overlook where we could help when it appeared overwhelming or not advantageous to our own wants and needs. So, I shared another story as a follow up.

On my phone, I pulled up the Parable of the Lost Sheep in the Gospel of Luke found in the Bible. I read the story Jesus told his followers about a shepherd who had a hundred sheep and one went missing. Instead of continuing to tend to the ninety-nine, the shepherd left to seek out the one missing. I asked the class if they would do the same.

Again, in unison they proclaimed they would. I challenged their answer this time.

"You would leave ninety-nine well mannered, rule-following sheep to find the one that went astray?"

"Absolutely," they shouted.

"But what if in doing so, the ninety-nine others went missing? Wouldn't it be better to have ninety-nine than one?"

They weren't taking my bait; instead, I knew they were telling me what I wanted to hear, not what they would likely have done. So, I proposed another scenario.

ON THE MARKER BOARD, I DREW A ONE-HUNDRED-DOLLAR BILL AND ASKED THE CLASS HOW MANY SINGLE DOLLARS IT WOULD TAKE TO HAVE A HUNDRED.

They liked considering what it would feel like to hold a hundred one-dollar bills in their hands, but they weren't too keen on my suggestion that the wind blew one out.

"To get the one dollar," I shared. "Would require you to put the ninety-nine down. Would you do it?" At this point, they began getting inventive.

"I'd put the ninety-nine under a rock to ensure they wouldn't fly away," one said.

"I have pockets, Mrs. Stephanie. I'll put the other in my pocket for safe keeping," a student proudly stated.

No one was willing to give up that dollar, so I offered one more situation for consideration. Next to the one-hundred-dollar bill I drew a dollar bill, asking the kids how many pennies it took to make one. They were onto my trick by this point, and quickly shouted a hundred. A hundred pennies are heavy, I reminded them, and together we put our hands up pretending to see how heavy that was.

"If one penny fell out, would you go after it?" I asked.

The mother of a student in class laughed while answering, "Only if it had landed heads up!"

While I appreciated their excitement for knowing the right answers—the ones that modeled Jesus's behavior—I fessed up, telling them that I wouldn't have gone for the single sheep.

I would have waved bye to the dollar because ninety-nine others were more than I had now. And I wouldn't have even noticed the penny. At that point, the faces of my students sunk, and they agreed that they, too, would probably do the same now that they were thinking about it more.

Jesus, I reminded them, cared for the one always. And we were called to follow in his footsteps.

The student's mother who had attended our class each week to support her son who was nonverbal autistic offered a reminder of the donations our class had offered up at Christmas. Together, thanks to the generosity of their families, friends and the community, we had created oodles of reusable bags filled to the brim with toiletries, nonperishable foods and winter necessities to give to the homeless in our community. Each student had left with a bag and a charge to seek out someone to gift it to.

AFTER ERASING THE FICTITIOUS BILLS, I WROTE THE WORD "TALENTS" ON THE MARKER BOARD.

I asked the kids to share their talents that they could use to help the one.

"I can become a baseball player and donate to the homeless," a kid proudly stated.

"I can play the piano and use it as a fundraiser to feed the poor," another replied.

After scribing the litany of their beautiful thoughts on the board, I heard a pause. I turned around and locked eyes with one of the girls sitting in the second row of desks. I could see the heaviness of her heart plastered on her face. "What comes to your mind?" I asked her, and she began her story.

There was a girl in her class who was hateful to everyone, she shared. No one liked her at all, and she was always the outcast during recess. Anytime someone said something to her, she would snap back with an attitude. The rest of the class made a name for her, and it was evident the girl in my class had allowed the words to slip through her lips before too. With utter sadness, she shared that that girl was one that everyone overlooked.

"How can I be nice to her, Mrs. Stephanie?" she asked. "Especially when she's mean to everyone?"

With age comes wisdom, I now know. But I was transported back to my elementary school days, remembering the "ones" who were outcast in my school too. While I attempted to invite them into my circles, inevitably, I would stop and move on with my life, unconcerned about what was happening in theirs.

"When someone is mean to you," I told her. "They likely have something else they are dealing with that you don't see. If everyone in school called you names, wouldn't you lash out?"

Everyone in class nodded in agreement, because she had uncovered a decision that was harder to make than running after the dollar. Leaving ninety-nine friends behind for the one outcast was no small feat for anyone to do. As a class, we brainstormed ways for their classmate to invite the not-so-nice student to play the following week, hopeful it would be a step in a direction of change.

When class concluded and I watched the second graders depart to enjoy the rest of their Sunday, I looked at Cory in awe of what we just experienced. A new seed was planted in all the kids, not because we had offered it, but because we created the conditions for it.

I would suspect that if Jesus had a seed packet filled with one hundred tiny seeds the size of a black ballpoint pen tip, he could care for each individually without focusing on the whole.

Instead of tossing them all in and hoping for the best, he would go searching for the one that slipped through the cracks between his fingers, knowing that seed had potential too. And, because of his diligence, all would grow.

If ninety-nine...
... of your seeds flourished, would you notice the one dud?
... plants survived, would you fret over the one the frost took?
... of your passions succeeded, would you ever try out another?
... people were inspired by your words, would you inspire another?
... days of your life had purpose, would you squander the hundredth?

Every seed has a purpose. Every person is worthy. Every plant has a mission. Every passion has potential. Every individual's voice deserves to be heard. Every word you say has an impact. Every day has meaning, and every life matters.

Don't neglect the one; go searching for it.

PART TWO

The Roots

We don't want our past to define us, but it does ground us.
We seek to eliminate some roots, but all serve a purpose.

Before a seed reaches its potential, it first establishes roots, preparing for the future by acknowledging its purpose which is refined through experiences that provide it the necessary tools needed to grow.

Every step you've made in life has meaning, shaping you while building an intricate foundation, a root system that is meant to help you weather storms ahead. Your family, your education, your experiences—both the monumental and the seemingly insignificant—are equally embedded in your root system.

Everything in life happens on purpose—preparing you, rooting you. The roots aren't your defining moments, but they are a part of your structure and a part of you, never to be forgotten even though they remain hidden.

They are the reason you are standing today.
And they will be the reason you are standing tomorrow too.

The Hike

I awoke to a sealed envelope with my name inscribed on it sitting on my dresser, eager to release its secret. The demands of the day prior left my body yearning for more sleep, so I embraced the fact that my youngest had decided it was a sleep-in kind of day too. Before he could make his presence known by barging into the bedroom, I gave the envelope the opportunity to fulfill its duty, and upon opening it revealed a message my husband had written.

Pack a bag... you deserve a break. We are leaving tonight for a surprise adventure.

If anyone knew me better than myself, it was my better half. So, when he told me I needed a break, I listened, for he usually detected it before I could. That evening, after tucking our three littles to bed at their grandparents' house, we hopped in the car, and he drove me to a secret place only he knew the address of. For once, the end destination didn't matter. I knew I was in for a journey, and I fully embraced it.

The night deepened, and the stars proudly emerged as the car slowed to weave cautiously through windy curves up a large hill I could only expect would have stressed this "fearer of heights" out during the daytime. As we drew near to our destination, I found solace in the belief that sometimes ignorance is bliss and relaxed in the truth that whatever was around the next turn was worth it.

The promise of seeing a watercolor painting in the morning sky as the sun peeked over the horizon filled me with anticipation. As we reached the welcome sign to General Butler State Resort Park, my joy knew no bounds. I had visited this park before, years prior when I was in a different job and a different headspace. But I was excited for the much-needed restful quiet time, the slower pace the country offered and the promise of outdoor photography could do for my perspective. Just me, my husband, my camera and my hiking boots were the makings of a getaway to remember.

CORY WAS ACUTELY AWARE THAT I NEEDED A GOOD,
RIGOROUS HIKE, BUT I WASN'T.

It wasn't apparent to me how much my soul needed the deliberate break and the ease of an outdoor air inhale, or how much my body ached for outdoor exploration. I wasn't aware how critical that pause was in my life until I took it; not until the next morning when we bundled up and embarked on a morning hike.

Some prefer a surprise trip to a major city where the night scene could drown out the week's worries. Others savor a day soaking at a spa or the clanging of slot machines becoming their white noise during a trip to the nearest casino. Peace and quiet is found in different nooks and crannies. For me, it happens best when I'm outside, one with nature, with the freedom to explore and a chance to disconnect.

We should have known we were in for an unforgettable experience when we struggled to find the hike's entrance. It promised us five miles of exercise coupled with several sightseeing opportunities perfect for satisfying my photographer's eye. What more could I ask for? But the hidden path to nowhere quickly revealed its true nature, leaving me chilled to the bone and my legs weary. I begged the wind for a winter blanket, stronger muscles and a flatter trail to trek.

Reasonable requests, one might say.
But hidden on a little-known trail in a state park, my pleas went unnoticed.

Cory and I used this time to talk about life—our kids, our new house build, our upcoming projects at work—as a deviation tactic from the weekend's unexpected intensity. It was easy to converse while walking downhill, as each step was effortless thanks to gravity. But, as with most hikes and most things in life, what goes down must come up. The once welcoming hill had become my worst enemy, with nothing more than my wobbly legs and injured pride to carry me back up.

WITH EVERY STEP UP THE STEEP INCLINE, MY AUDIBLE VOICE DECREASED IN PITCH AND FREQUENCY.

At first, all I heard were birds singing in the nearby maple trees amid my quick breaks and pounding heartbeat. I attempted to focus my thoughts on embracing their beautiful music as an anthem for a self-titled album they were writing for me, offering notes of encouragement to help me persevere. I searched for any distraction to alleviate the pain in my legs, while coaching them to continue the climb and combat the fatigue that was quickly spreading through my body. My audible voice may have been silenced, but my inner voice was in high gear.

You know that voice; the one that lives within you, helping discern situations, evaluate gut reactions and has the power to propel you or the power to break you.

This voice can build you up or rip you to shreds. It can be your number one fan or your own worst enemy.

On that day, mine doubted whether I had enough determination to make it up that hill. *I wasn't good enough*, it said on repeat. *Your legs are giving up.*

That voice may have been right, I considered. Maybe my legs weren't made for the steep incline; maybe I wasn't going to be able to complete this hike. But I was good enough, I knew, and instead of listening to her, I kept going anyway. I didn't stop until my audible voice spoke something more profound than I originally noticed.

"THANK HEAVENS FOR THE ROOTS."

I hadn't a clue "the how" of the charge I had just declared. I was going to get up that hill come hell or high water, but it would take a miracle. I began to use my arms to brace my legs with each step they took, and right before I was about to beg my husband to carry me like he would our children, I looked down to notice the help I had been praying for.

It had been a sloshy, wet kind of hike. As if the incline wasn't challenging enough, couple it with uneven ground and leftover remnants of a rainy day before and the challenge was more than tough for this not-so-in-shape gal. I would have stopped if it weren't for the roots; the strong tree roots that grounded the tree itself were also stabilizing me.

As I expressed gratitude to the root systems around me, I had a sudden realization of why my husband brought me to this park, on this day and to this hike. Nothing on its path was coincidental—not the valleys that lead to the beautiful scenic peak, not the depleting path which pushed us to travel on uncharted territory and definitely not the five deer that stood in awe of us just as we were standing in awe of them.

Noticing the roots around me, I realized how my past experiences were supporting me through my current challenges and future ones too. For years later, I uncovered a chronic health condition at the root of my fatigue that very day.

Each root I stepped over, through and on top of was a visual reminder of past hurdles, beautiful perspective-shaping moments and my strong foundation of values that would help me stand strong amid any storm brewing.

MY ROOT SYSTEM WAS PURPOSEFUL, GIVING ME THE ADDITIONAL STRENGTH NEEDED FOR EACH STEP OF MY LIFE'S HIKE. AND YOURS IS TOO.

When I stopped looking down where my feet were stepping, I noticed that the path was leading me, not me leading it. Unexpectedly, but by God's beautiful design, Cory had picked a dreary day for our hike. Very little life was found on our trail, until I noticed the only glimpse of greenery among the multitude of brown was the luscious, living moss befriending the roots and paving the way. If I stopped questioning each step I took and trusted the journey, I would have noticed sooner that the path was, is and always will be clear, purposeful and a welcoming invitation for all.

I gained much more than sore hips and a blister on my big toe during that surprise weekend-getaway hike. I left with a camera full of memories and a soul replenished, reminding me that it's equally important to be grateful for your roots as it is to look ahead to future growth because where you've been can give you the strength you need to traverse the path awaiting ahead.

The Hostas

I stood there speechless, in awe of the living painting before me. My family had piled in our van that afternoon to visit the nearby plant nursery, only a mile or so from our home, with the intention of adding some color to our landscape. I was taken aback by the vast selection of colors spanning every shade of a prism and the varieties that stretched beyond the limits of my sight.

I made a mental note that if I had a choice as to what heaven would be like, I would choose to fall into forever here, in this.

Every inch of the greenhouse was painted in flower blooms; it was a rainbow that didn't disappear, one you could easily touch and vagrantly smell. Like my favorite scene from the movie *What Dreams May Come* starring Robin Williams, I yearned to run from corner to corner dancing among the annuals.

I credit my mom for my love of begonias and petunias, two flowers that are welcomed into our flower beds each year, adding pink and purple spice to the lush greenery. As a kid, my mom and I would select our favorites and fill two pots framing our entryway with them. We turned their growth into a daily contest, seeing whose pot of beauty would flourish the quickest. Inevitably, it would be hers since she already had a green thumb. It took me a few more years to discover mine, and when I unearthed that, coincidentally, mine was green because I have a knack for caring for plants. When it comes to flowers, however, my abilities are somewhat questionable.

THERE IS MUCH I CHERISH ABOUT THE FIRST HOME CORY AND I HAD TOGETHER.

Perfectly situated on Blackberry Circle, our home had plenty of space for a garden, which was a must-have on our requirement list. Hardwood floors gave its insides character, and while the open floor plan was atypical for its building era, it was perfect for our love of hosting gatherings. A single fruit tree proudly perched in the front yard, just outside of our daughter's bedroom, and the kitchen had an instant hot water gadget, perfect for heating up frozen milk for middle of the night meals when the kids were newborn.

This home was where Cory and I celebrated the news of each pregnancy, and where we fell into sorrow's deep depths after the loss of our oldest. It's where our children took their first steps and where we got our collective footing on parenting.

The walls could tell stories of life-changing conversations, sleepless nights of worry, belly laughs that were contagious and immense growth for everyone who slept under its roof.

When life felt like too much to handle, I could be found cuddled with a kid under the shade the back porch offered, observing the life that lived right outside our back door. More than just our family called this space home. Cardinals frequently visited, and butterflies fluttered among the dandelion weeds. Carpenter bees had a love for our porch's wood, annually creating annoying nests within it. Since we didn't have a dog yet, the neighborhood rabbits preferred our fenced yard where their family could live hidden in the grass, unexposed to breathing predators. In the mornings, the momma nursed her littles, breathing sighs of relief knowing her babies were safe and food was near, being that our garden was just a hop away.

Our backyard required minimal landscaping. The previous owners had planted a thriving hosta garden that edged our pebbled walk to the fence, which was one of my favorite touches to the space. Each year, their presence would prove that growth can be seasonal, and just because something appears dead, it could surprise you. The hostas were all up in each other's business. Planted closely from the get-go, they had taken over every inch of their plot of dirt, outwardly showing their gratitude through purple offshoots of joy.

After planting begonias in the front landscape and the petunias in our porch flower pots that day, I walked around the house's perimeter to ensure I didn't miss an opportunity to add a bit of color to the backyard. The hostas were in full bloom.

There was no taming their happiness or no room to add begonias. Loud and proud, they enjoyed their siloed community, except for one that appeared to be crying for help.

AT THE END OF THE LINEUP WAS A PEAKED HOSTA. IT EAGERLY REACHED FOR THE SUN, BUT ITS LEAVES WEREN'T QUITE AS STEADY AS THE REST OF ITS FAMILY.

The black mulch had been maneuvered away from its base, and a bit of dirt left a trail on the walkway to the culprit of the conundrum. Like a detective in the movie *Sherlock Gnomes*, I began investigating.

Maybe a kid accidentally explored the flower bed, I thought while inviting the soil back to the base of the plant. As I patted the soil in like tucking a kid into bed at night, the mulch collapsed unexpectedly into the land. It was as if it was holding together by a hair and my pressure broke it. Confused, I grabbed the hosta to pull its leaves to the side, and in doing so, the plant gave up and fell into my hands.

No longer in the soil, the once thriving plant laid lifeless in my palms. The leaves were still green, but the roots were nonexistent.
It was working in overdrive, but ran out of steam and nourishment.

Where the roots should have been was a small hollow tunnel instead. I followed the path, realizing the hosta's neighbor was doomed. I touched its base, and it too fell over, helplessly crying out. Down the row I went, following the unwanted and underground pathway. Each plant led to the same demise. Whatever had built the tunnel had eaten each and every root.

Over a dozen hostas laid lifeless on the concrete when Cory came around the corner with his gardening gloves on and a heavy bag of fresh mulch.

Having thought I just made the conscious decision to reinvent the flower bed after evicting the hostas, he was ready for whatever I had up my sleeves. My face told a different story; I was heartbroken that I couldn't save these plants or their roots.

After chatting with neighbors, we learned of a new critter that had made our yard their home without asking permission. Voles. Also known as field mice, voles are relatives of hamsters, pets I had plenty of growing up. Inside, they were cute. Outside, they were destructive. At first I thought we had moles, but I uncovered their distinctive differences.

Moles eat pesky insects.

Voles eat beloved plants, and they had devoured mine.

I sat on the walkway in tears, hugging my hostas and all the bugs that were hidden within. I had loved their annual beauty and their passion for living. I let them down without even knowing. They tried to give their all, but without roots, they didn't stand a chance.

Life isn't possible without a foundation. No matter the beauty above the dirt, if nothing is below, their attempts for growth fell short.

I left that space vacant that year. It was a season of mourning, and each day I tinkered in the vegetable garden, I glanced at the naked space where the hostas once were. It felt bare and wrong, like a graveyard of sorts. But I didn't have answers to prevent another massacre, and I wasn't ready for that misery again. Instead, I filled in the tunnels, omitted the voles' vegetation and prayed they would magically become extinct.

THE NEXT SPRING, I SNATCHED UP FOUR KNOCKOUT ROSE BUSHES ALONG WITH THE BEGONIAS AND PETUNIAS.

The rose bushes not only resembled my feelings—part thorny curmudgeon and part strikingly hopeful—but they also symbolized our children, our three that we hug daily and our one that patiently awaits a reunion in heaven. The bushes were small but mighty, but I knew their roots because I was a part of them.

Let the voles attempt to gnaw at these suckers, I thought.

This momma bear is ready to fight for their roots.

Nearly a decade later, when all our memories were packed in cardboard moving boxes, I visited the backyard for the last time. I debated digging up the thriving rose bushes for relocation to our new home, but their roots were strong and mighty, declaring this place as their forever residence. I knew they could make it without me now, for their thorns had poked me a time or two when attempting to prune too much or snip a bloom too early. Each time I laughed, realizing that it was time for this helicopter mom to step back and let them take over. They were ready to flourish on their own, thanks to their strong roots.

As we drove away, a trailer hitched to our SUV filled to the brim with children's toys and furniture, I smiled reflecting on all the hostas and the roses had taught me.

WE ALL NEED ROOTS.

They stabilize us while at the same time grounding us. I smirked, reminiscing about the times my kids were sent to their rooms to reflect on their out-of-line behaviors. Hopefully one day they would realize those learnings offer a stabilizing foundation.

They nourish us from below so we can show our true and beautiful colors. By offering wisdom, all I can hope is that my kids don't make the same mistakes I do. But if and when they do, I will be there to help push the soil back around their base once more.

They anchor us in truth so that when the harsh realities of the world are exposed, they never forget who or whose they are. They are always ours, and they will forever be His. Like a ship anchored in raging waters, my hope is that the anchor holds strong, offering strength when they feel like they have little.

They offer support, and we all need that from time to time. Like the once interwoven root system that the hostas had, when we come together we can do more, be more and grow more. Community deepens our roots, and when they are tightly bound together, everyone thrives.

Even when roots are destroyed, the collective can persevere. Together, if I could have evicted the voles, maybe the hostas would have grown new roots because they had one another.

In the rearview mirror, I glanced back, knowing the roots we created as a family could be replanted wherever we landed next. Because we were together, and collectively, we could conquer anything.

The Picnic

I t was time. Actually it was long overdue. I had dodged the eyesore for weeks, but I could no longer ignore the challenge that sat before me. The tangled mess was ready to be free, even though I had no idea where to start. In the silence they beckoned, and no amount of running from them would quiet their collective plea. The bag of bare-root strawberries were ready. It was time to figure out how to wake them up.

The warmth and caffeine from my chai tea gave me the nudge that morning to open the twice-used plastic grocery bag and expose its contents. Fifty strawberry plants had been promised when I went in on a bulk purchase with a friend. I dreamed of spring outings to the garden where my family would gather homegrown goodness, too sweet to wait for enjoyment around the kitchen table. Instead, we'd plop on the rolling hills and let the strawberries' juice trickle down our chins as we enjoyed their deliciousness together.

These are the dreams of gardeners.
Bare-root plants live among the nightmares.

My friend had done her research. She knew what she had signed up for. I, on the other hand, was a bit too trusting and figured purchasing bare-root strawberry plants meant that they came with exposed roots without soil, which was not what I found when I peeked in the bag of tricks. Tricks sure felt like what I saw.

A few handfuls of dirt clumps.
Some left over and seemingly overlooked roots.
Not a single bit of green was found anywhere.

I was staring death in the face, questioning if we got scammed. This was absolutely not what I signed up for. I emptied the pile of waste on a baking sheet and discovered two measly leaves, but nothing more appeared to have promise. I was deflated before I even started, which didn't offer much hope to the lifeless plants before me. After getting a reassuring text from my partner in gardening crime that this was exactly what we ordered, I did some YouTube research to figure out what my next step should be. Surely I wouldn't just plop these bad boys into the ground and hope for the best.

The video I found was of a passionate gardener who, not only outlined the missing steps on bare-root planting, but also shared the why behind it. Glued to the video, my gardening knowledge expanded that day, which both helped with the future of my strawberry plants and my own personal growth too.

BARE-ROOT PLANTS ARE A GARDENING DISTRIBUTOR'S BEST OPTION TO OFFER A FINANCIAL WIN-WIN FOR EVERYONE.

The gardener on the video outlined how bare-root plants are uprooted in their dormant state, given a root bath to wash free any remaining soil and shipped to buyers for them to transplant into their gardens. While the in-between transition may cause the plants to look a bit withered, rough even, it's the most cost-effective option since they are lighter, making them cheaper to ship.

No pots are necessary. No soil was required. As long as the shipping window is during the dormant stage, everyone comes out winners—sellers, buyers and strawberries.

While that was a desired outcome, the gardener's next point was even more poignant. When you take it to the root, you are less likely to have hitchhikers. I knew that you never wanted to pick up a hitchhiker on the interstate; my dad had ingrained that in me at a young age. However, the day my grandma and I found ourselves stranded with a broken car on the side of a busy road prior to the cell phone age, I was grateful others didn't abide by the advice I had been taught. Some hitchhikers are dangerous, but we weren't.

I learned that hitchhiker was another word for an invasive plant that hitched a ride on another plant without approval. Those could be dangerous, bringing in weeds and other unwanted sprouts to your strawberry patch. Knowing the challenge we already experienced with invasive weeds, I was grateful to not have others. Without my knowing, the strawberry plant seller was thinking about the strawberry plant buyer!

BEFORE PLANTING, HOWEVER, THE STRAWBERRIES NEEDED AND DESERVED A WARM BATH.

I could commiserate. After a long day, a bath always did the trick for me. These plants had been pulled from their home, stripped of their warmth and stuck in a bag for a long ride to their destination. They were tired and thirsty, and a bath does everyone's soul some good, strawberries included. I prepared a kitchen bowl with lukewarm tap water and allowed the plants to show me their backstrokes and how long they could hold their breath underwater.

The warm bath did more than reinvigorate the plants; it separated the good from the no longer needed. The bare-root plants were exposed, and the dirt fell to the wayside. What helped the strawberries get here was no longer necessary to get to their final destination. An hour later, as I lifted each from the bath and patted them dry, I noticed next to each crown was a green leaf, perfectly awoken and proudly ready. Finally, I was too.

They had a purpose: to populate our garden.
I had a goal: to enjoy the fruits of their labor.
Together: we were going to make magic.

Fifty mini pots sat on our back porch with strawberry plants held within while we prepared to till the garden and welcome them home. Each morning before the sun peeked over the horizon and each afternoon once the sun had begun to set, I would offer them a drink, celebrating their growth and acknowledging mine too. Within a day, they showed signs of life. Within several, many had multiple leaves join in the celebration. What appeared to be dead had been anything but. They were more than just awake; they were ready to grow.

I had grown strawberries before but never bare-root plants. In our previous garden, we had purchased plant starters from the nursery at the end of strawberry season. The plants already looked healthy, and that year we enjoyed a late-crop harvest. And, having little knowledge about strawberries then, I saw their tendency to get a bit unwieldy.

As I planted these fifty, I anxiously awaited them to run, literally. Strawberries are known to create runners, new sprouts that grow from seemingly delicate extended stems.

Once those stems stretch just enough outside of their comfort zone to find a new place to land, the plant will create new roots, new leaves and a new plant altogether.

STRAWBERRIES ARE LIVING, BREATHING REMINDERS OF
FAMILY TREES.

As the plant runs, so does their lineage. You can see their connections
to each other, and tracing their heritage back to their originations is a
favorite pastime of mine. They are sneaky too. Without your knowing, they will create an offshoot that you could unintentionally squash
if you aren't careful. They require regular care, as do most families.
And while runners can get a bit unruly if you let them, a little guidance will help home gardeners create thick and fruitful patches that
offer plenty of berries for families and rabbits alike.

The best gardens take time, and patience is the desired soft skill of
a gardener.

It could take years for the soil to be perfected, a garden to have
adequate irrigation and for strawberries to come into their own. Each
year around the sun is a step closer to our desired garden. And every
year I learn a bit more about the garden as a whole, the plants individually and myself along the way.

I'll never forget the day the kids and I squealed with excitement when
we found the first batch of berries that hadn't yet been nibbled on by
the rabbits. We had lost earlier ones to the critters living off the land
with us, but this time, we beat them to the sweet punch. Meticulously,
we picked each we could find, fitting our entire harvest in one tiny
child's palm.

Together, we found the perfect spot on the rolling hill alongside our
garden for a petit picnic of two to three strawberries each. With every
bite, we relished the cherished taste of homegrown love. The warm
juiciness was just what I dreamed of, but the time together was even
sweeter.

The Power

~~~

Even though we didn't ask him to, he came anyway. We had dialed the number clearly noted on the For Sale by Owner sign waving in the wind in front of the property we would later call ours. After a few rings, the man on the other side of the phone answered our inquiry on acreage and pricing, both of which were more than we had desired and our budget had capacity for. Persistently, however, the owner encouraged us to give him five minutes and he'd take us on a tour of the property.

I wondered if we should bail prior to his arrival, before the hook was lodged and we digested the bait. Having seen my knees wobble during a timeshare tour of a condo we never wanted but were nearly conned into investing in, I knew that I had little self-control and couldn't be trusted.

My heart was already saying yes, but my head was attempting to persuade it otherwise. Inevitably, my heart won.

The property's current owner pulled up in a farm truck and invited us to hop in the back so he could show us every inch of the land. I guess with the fresh air came newfound trust in people you had never met but followed their not-so-subtle commands anyway. Without question, we hopped into the truck bed as Marvin introduced himself after pulling back the sliding window that separated us. With every bump we drove over and twist we went around, I fell more in love with the space. But it was the hike to the creek that sealed the deal.

MOST OF THE TWENTY-FIVE-AND-A-HALF-ACRE LOT WAS ROLLING HILLS AND PREVIOUS COW PASTURES.

Two spring-fed ponds were precisely situated where the land connected in the valleys. On the left of the property was a herd of cattle watching our every move while attempting to sing their out-of-tune baritone *moos*. On the right was a horse pasture that butted up to the property, with three majestic creatures poetically grazing, occasionally observing our presence. The front pond's overflow created a shallow creek bed that weaved through a tree line into the back-woods, which followed along the right-side property line to meet up at a creek deeper in the woods, or at least that was what Marvin promised.

The truck came to a halt on the property beyond where the sound of driving cars could be heard or cell service was available. Not wanting to disappoint Marvin's eagerness, Cory and I obliged to his request to show us the creek that could only be traveled to by foot. The back portion of the land was wooded, but a well-manicured path eased our descent. Later, I learned that Marvin frequented this place often and held cherished memories with family and friends there. The steep incline down required me to walk sideways to keep a steady grip. I was too excited for the hike down to ever think about the energy I'd need to get back up. But, as promised, the destination was worth the journey.

Hidden on the farthest part of the property was a bubbling creek, dancing around gorgeous creek stone and shaded by hundred-year-old oaks and evergreens. Visited by deer (as well as coyotes and snakes, although I preferred to avoid considering them), this place was the pure essence of peace and tranquility.

It was where spa music was recorded, where artists sought inspiration and where our kids would make memories, I determined.

Hopping from stone to stone, Marvin guided us from one side of the freshwater creek to the other, navigating downed trees so he could reveal the property line while divulging his dreams for the land. While he and my husband discussed specifics, I created distance, lagging behind them to tune out the discussion and soak in the moment. The crawdads nervously dodged my steps, bouncing between the rocks like a ball in a pinball machine. The temperature shifted by degrees, thanks to the towering trees hiding us from the sun's rays. And I became keenly aware of the tree line and its intricate root system.

On one side of the creek was a flat patch of green grass and wildflowers, a place that would make a picturesque picnic spot. On the other was exposed roots and about a ten-foot drop from the soil to the creek. Marvin observed my curiosity, explaining that while the creek was calm that day, a healthy rainfall always caused rising water levels. What was currently safe to explore could take a turn quickly. Over time and with more downpours, the water was slowly eroding away the soil. The roots, however, were holding it all in place.

"You see that tree," Marvin pointed out. It was one somewhat leaning that someone might consider removing. "Leave it be. Its roots are among others that are helping to hold it together."

Upon further inspection, I could see the pact that the trees had made. They loved their home, and they wouldn't give it up if their life depended upon it. It actually did. Hand in hand, root woven with root, they were the unified reason for the hill's remaining form. The power of the roots kept all well, and to this day, still does. Water levels rise and the crystal-clear waters gush, but outside of new creek stone as a heavy rain's parting gift, the soil remains because the powerful roots hang on to their friend with all their might.

I WAS INDOCTRINATED TO THE IMMENSE POWER OF ROOTS WHEN CORY RECEIVED A PHONE CALL FROM OUR NEIGHBOR.

We were living in our first home at the time, where neighbors were within earshot, although ours were respectful of boundaries and rarely reached out for anything more than friendly waves as we all came and went. The call was out of character, and immediately, I suspected the worst.

Our neighbor owned a leak detection company and could spot a leak with merely his nose at times. He noticed something off in our front yard and put Cory on a goose chase to explore the culprit. As suspected, a gas leak was underway, one we would have never known about until too late. He saved us, but we couldn't save the trees.

The lone fruit tree was the highlight of my front yard. In the spring, when it came out of hibernation, it produced the most eye-catching magenta blooms I'd ever seen. Covered in radiance and swaying with the wind it would appear to be on fire, with the flames being deep shades of pink instead of hues of orange. To fix the gas leak, an excavator had to open up our yard and expose the culprit, the roots of this treasured tree and the evergreen in our shrubbery.

Wrapped around the pipes, it resembled the kids who couldn't help but hug kittens a tad too tight, except the kittens could hopefully escape and the pipes weren't quite as nimble.

The roots followed the pipe's path like a child follows their parent: extremely close and with vigor. In partnership with the fruit tree, the evergreen in our landscaping had followed suit, offering the pipe double damage.

We lost the trees, but we didn't lose the house, or worse, any of us.

The bare spot in the yard was covered in sod, and a magnolia tree was planted in place of the evergreen. Butterfly-attracting shrubs filled in the remaining landscaping gaps, and I found my daughter sitting next to them one morning while we were out watering the flowers. When asked what she was doing so close to the bushes, she shared that she was breathing in their beauty and watching the bees do their work.

Her wisdom was nearly as powerful as the roots proved to be. While roots prevent erosion, perspective prevents internal depletion. While roots can break pipes, words can open them. While roots are adaptable, following with precision, we are too. Our adaptability, however, shapes us, not shatters us.

Roots can hold us or break us.
They can define us or refine us.
They can steady us or derail us.

We grow with them, from them and because of them. The important ones prevent erosion, but the unhealthy ones could have us in a death grip. Knowing when to lean on them and when to break free from them is our challenge. And finding beauty to breathe in along the way is our charge.

The Freedom

L ike any newly married couple with the world as their oyster, we saw our first backyard as a yard of possibilities. One day we'd have a trampoline for the littles we dreamed of to play on. We'd have a swing where we would push them high into the clouds. A pool would be a welcomed addition to cut in half the summer's heat. And the garden would bear the most delicious fruits of our labor.

Our slice of heaven would be memorable, no matter the life season.

Fresh on the other side of college and navigating two mortgages since our condo was taking longer to sell than we hoped, the equity we had to pour into the yard couldn't be found in our pockets; instead, it was found in our free labor. We had a shovel and a vision and youthful energy to pair with it. Since kids weren't on the horizon quite yet, the garden was our first project, and it came with no directions (kids didn't either, we found out a year later!).

THE SOD WAS THICK, OBVIOUSLY CONSISTENTLY FERTILIZED
BY THE HOME'S PREVIOUS OWNER.

Each day that year in late spring we took turns attempting to rip
through the grass's fibrous roots to expose the top soil underneath.
Our home sat on a quarter-acre lot, and our backyard was a blank
canvas, but we opted for a twelve-foot by twelve-foot space to do our
first family planting.

After little progress in sod removal, my dad rented a sod cutter for the
day, which promised to turn our hopes for a garden into a reality. On
paper, the plot looked massive. But after removing the sod, and
muscle aches from it, we were surprised by how little it really was.

For the first year, however, we figured it would work. Our
muscles, on the other hand, begged us to not second guess our
decision.

Not far from our home was our county extension office, which
offered free soil sampling and several in-person learning opportunities for both the seasoned gardener who wanted to perfect their
orchard or the newbie like me, unsure of the first step to take. I
learned all about canning during one of their classes, and each year, I
eagerly awaited their plant sale. Farmers from all over the county and
beyond would gather one day every April to sell their prized posses-
sions, plant starters of all kinds. Rain or shine, I was always one of the
first to arrive and would spend hours navigating a handful of tents.

It was there I discovered unique varieties such as chocolate cherry
tomatoes and crimson watermelons. Inevitably, I'd arrive home with
more plants than our garden had space for but always accommodated
nonetheless.

THAT YEAR, MY GRANDPA LOANED US HIS TILLER SO WE COULD PREPARE THE SOIL FOR PLANTING.

He joined my dad in bringing it over as he was eager to see what our land could produce and was proud of passing down his love of gardening to another generation. He eyed up the flats of tomatoes and peppers we had cooling on the back porch and began a friendly annual competition to see who would pick the first tomato. He always won.

Dictating from the sidelines, my dad and grandpa coached Cory on how deep to till the soil for best outcomes. Ours was like clay that first year, but because of the advice they shared, over time it became desirable by all. After several rounds of using the tiller to break up the land, Cory was ready to put in the first plant, a tomato I'm sure. Although I grew up gardening, my husband's dad had not passed down his passion for it to him. Despite his parents growing tomatoes and peppers in pots on their apartment balcony, Cory never took interest and was inexperienced.

As he extracted the tomato starter from its plastic transporting pot, my grandpa offered some advice. "You see the low leaves close to the roots?" he drew his attention to. "Be sure to pinch them off. You want your plants to grow tall and strong. The nutrients will go to the lowest leaves first, but you want it to go to the strongest ones." Cory followed directions and pinched off the tiny leaf closest to the tomato's roots.

"Before you put the plant in the soil," he continued. "Be sure to break up the roots a bit as well. This will encourage them to grow best."

With one hand gently holding the tomato's stalk, Cory used his other to free the roots entangled around the soil. To his surprise, what initially appeared to only be a couple of inches of roots were much longer once freed from their tangled mess. The plant was now ready, and Cory had the honor of welcoming it to its new home in the soil.

GRANDPA'S ADVICE WASN'T MEANT FOR TOMATO PLANTS ALONE. IT HOLDS MERIT FOR ALL PLANTS, INDOOR OR OUT.

After my grandma passed, my grandpa's forever sweetheart, our home was filled with plants of sympathy. Grateful for the thoughts and prayers that accompanied each, my favorite two were the ones I picked out. After our nuptials, Cory and I remained deeply connected with our florist. She was always on our short list of recommendations when people asked about their wedding musts, and anytime we needed a plant or flower, she was our go-to.

Between selecting the Scriptures and hymns for Grandma's funeral and gathering ingredients for a Thanksgiving meal we were preparing for the rest of my family to enjoy at the funeral home, I reached out to Carolyn, sharing ideas of what my mom and I wanted in each of our sympathy arrangements. Flowers lose their beauty after a week or so, and while I know peace lilies are the plant that never dies, this gal always kills them. I wanted a prayer plant, succulents and greenery that I could put around the house afterward in honor and memory of a woman who was deeply loved and loved deeply in return.

What she created were masterpieces, and the arrangements were the talk of day. I'm confident Grandma "oohed" and "aahed" in spirit as well. Weeks afterward, I still was.

I noticed the prayer plant in the middle of one of the arrangements, however, was becoming lifeless. While the plant was known to move throughout the day, getting its name for the opening of its leaves in the morning and the closing of them in the evening like its saying its nighttime prayers, it was dropping more than it ever should. I suspected it needed some room to grow on its own.

I collected some pots we had stored in the laundry room and ripped open a bag of potting soil to prepare for the transition of several plants in the arrangement. The prayer plant beautifully perked up in its new pot, grateful for the extra wiggle room. But before planting the succulent, I decided to move my thanksgiving cactus into a new pot so I could use the vacated pot, which appeared to be a better fit for the succulent. Upon lifting the cactus, I noticed the reason it was stagnant; it was root bound.

With nowhere to go, the roots were on the verge of giving up. They had grown to maximize its space, but no more room was available.

It was stuck, and without the need for its pot, I would never have known. It had outgrown its container, but hadn't been given the chance for change. Knowing plants can hear our words, I apologized profusely and settled it into a larger space with more room to spread its wings and fly, or grow in this case. Within the month, I barely noticed the cactus because it had nearly doubled.

ALONGSIDE MY GRANDPARENTS, ROOTS ARE SOME OF LIFE'S BEST TEACHERS.

For growth of any kind to happen, adequate space is needed. I quickly learned in our vegetable garden that either the plot needed doubling or I needed to scale back my plant starter purchase each year. We opted to triple the size of the garden the next year! I am now keenly aware of my houseplants, too, watching for halted growth, realizing it likely means it's root bound and ready for a new adventure in a different pot.

While our roots are meant to stabilize us, if we don't break them up a bit before planting, they won't extend far and wide, deepening our foundation and enabling us to grow stronger in the process. Giving our roots a gentle massage to break up the tangled mess may be scary, uncomfortable even, but it may offer the difference between surviving and thriving… getting by or flourishing.

There is freedom in breaking free from what we know, resting in the truth our roots offer and branching out to new places and new spaces.

PART THREE

The Breakthrough

A seed's growth is not based on its desire, but rather the nourishment it's offered. With the right conditions, it's given a chance.

To thrive, it needs hugs from the sun for energy and nutrients from the soil for growth. The rain's heavy downpours quenches its thirst. Even when these factors work together in unison, it still requires unwavering perseverance to navigate obstacles in order to break through the soil. Luckily, as it timidly emerges beyond its comfort zone, its roots are there to support its leap of faith.

True breakthroughs, for you or a seed, require more than what meets the eye. When knee-deep in manure, remember that those moments could hold you down or help you grow stronger roots, providing stability for future challenges. Hardships can help you weather storms that are coming, offering unexpected strength when needed most.

If a seed has the courage to stretch, giving growth a fighting chance…
If it can embrace the muck it's living under, seeing it as fertilizer…
If it can grow despite the odds against it…
If a seed can break through… you can too.

The Rocks

~∂∞⌣

It had been a long day, and she could sense my exhaustion just by looking at me. It was painted on my face, not with oil pastels or watercolors but charcoal present in dark circles from little sleep. Working long hours and trying to navigate a wide world of unknowns in the beginning of the pandemic had already started taking a toll on me, and it was only day one of the social distancing requirement that our community was experiencing.

I was tired; there was no denying it.
I was worried; there was no running from it.
I was unsure; there was no certainty anywhere.

I plopped on the couch, which had become my safety net from any and all concerns. There was something peaceful about being on the plush sofa cushions, resting my worries on the feather pillows while binge watching a guilty pleasure of a true crime docuseries or the latest suspense or sci-fi flick on Netflix. With the couch absorbing my stress and my mind vegging out on mindless content, I could tune out the noise wherever it came from most.

THAT NIGHT WAS LIKE MOST.

I found my spot in the corner of the sectional, rested my head on the pile of pillows perfectly situated and prepared for the impending slumber I was about to drift into.

That is, until she found me.

It's like her internal radar goes off when I'm not feeling my best. My little Lyndi—who wasn't so little anymore—found her way to the couch and wiggled to get as close to me as humanly possible. At the precise time that I needed her, she found me. I didn't realize she needed me too.

The two of us hugged in silence on the couch of safety for what felt like eternity, even though it was probably just short of a minute or two, but when I let up on my grip, hers tightened and she whispered: "Momma, I never want this moment to end. I want to hug you forever."

"Me too" was all that my full heart could express. "Me too."

Somehow, my daughter always knows my heart's desires before I do. She can peer into my soul and deliver a sweet message when I'm on the verge of tears or a hug just when I need it. She knows the words to say that fill me up when my cup feels quite empty, and she uses her ability for good to change the lives of everyone around her. That day, I needed her reminder of the power of a moment.

She's never been a big gift buyer; for years she only had a piggy bank of coins that would allow her to do so. She didn't understand all the nuances of what the world was experiencing in the thick of a pandemic, for she was just a little six-year-old-girl, and this momma tried everything to shield her and her brothers from worries too big for their hearts to carry just yet. But she didn't let any of that stop her from delivering ordinary miracles in the lives of those she interacted with, and she used what she had and what she knew to change others from the inside out.

The night prior, the two of us were cleaning out her room when I stumbled upon her "bags of goodies." These bags weren't filled with sweet treats or unique toys; instead they were filled to the brim with what most would consider junk. For as long as I could remember, Lyndi had collected what others would deem as garbage to use as gifts for people she met. She collected fallen flowers from the local craft stores to give as gifts in birthday bags. She collected instruction manuals so she could use it as paper to write you a message or draw you a flower. But that night I found her rocks.

Yes, rocks. Plain, gray rocks were weighing down her many purses. She had not collected them for their unique shape or design. Instead, she enjoyed their beauty, she told me. She celebrated the quantity she had collected over their unique qualities, for there were none. They all resembled one another—boring, gray lumps of nothing. She loved her rock collection though, because she saw what others didn't, something beautiful and miraculous in each.

WHILE I DIDN'T APPRECIATE HER ROCK COLLECTION, I DID HAVE ONE OF MY OWN.

After the first year of planting our garden on our new farm and harvesting very little, my dad was determined to make some adjustments. I knew our decreased bounty was due to our inability to nurture the land—failing to omit the weeds nightly and identify the need for extra watering quickly enough. We were in the middle of the house build, and our temporary living situation was over forty-five minutes away. It wasn't economically feasible to visit the garden daily. After a few weeks, we gave up and considered the produce a gift to the critters that would soon become our neighbors.

You reap what you sow as long as you care for what you sow too.

But that didn't appease my dad. He was confident the rolling hill contributed to the problem. The rain water didn't hold, running down to the pond instead of soaking into the soil, he believed.

So the following year, he hauled in more dirt than one could imagine needing to create a more level terrain and give our garden a fighting chance. He wanted juicy tomatoes for his BLT sandwiches as much as we wanted them for our homemade salsa and pasta sauce.

That year, though, the rain mocked our attempts, beginning to erode the edges of the newly exposed soil from the haul. Quickly, we needed a plan, and I concocted one to propose. I had wanted to use the onslaught of rock hidden in our creek bed for our fireplace. I learned that its weight would require additional support beams in the basement, and I wasn't willing to haul as much stone as they needed up the steep hill by foot. At this point, however, we had purchased Rosie, our handy UTV that had no problem driving any part of the farm's rugged terrain.

"What if we stacked creek rock around the garden?" I proposed to my husband, suggesting maybe it would not only prevent erosion but also create a beautiful visual addition to our dreamy backyard.

A gift given by each heavy rain, for any creek rock that was borrowed, two were returned in its place. It took years for us to slowly gather enough to cover half of the garden's perimeter, but within those years, we enjoyed hearty tomatoes of all shapes and sizes, kale in droves and the best green peppers ever tasted. We cried cutting onions we picked and used our cucumber pickings to make homemade Benedictine dip and bread and butter pickles.

THE ROCKS WERE OUR RESCUE, AND THEY WERE HERS TOO.

Lyndi saw their worth years before I ever did. She saw beauty in what I saw as boring. She found a uniqueness before I noticed their varying shapes that would fit perfectly like a puzzle to offer the garden support. She made something from nothing, inspiring me to find a solution using what was originally overlooked.

Because of the rocks surrounding our garden, our plants experience annual breakthroughs.

Because of her perspective of rocks and everything else she touches, she inspires us to break through.

Rocks may break windows, but they are now subtle reminders to me that breaks leave messages; breakthroughs create growth. What has the power to break you can empower you to break through too.

The Mountains

❧

I had become numb to the world around me. It felt like everyone wanted something from me, but I had very little if anything to offer back to those vying for a piece.

My kids had demands, as did the rest of my family. My clients had needs, all being demanded for at once. The workload was more than anyone could handle alone, even though I tried.

I was not just any sort of tired; I was soul tired. And I had hit rock bottom.

I wanted to run away.

I had contemplated moving to Hawaii and changing my name; at least there I would bask in the sun while I hid from Overwhelm and Anxiety. But underneath my fight or flight response was a woman just utterly exhausted, and I needed to recharge.

CORY KNEW I NEEDED A CHANGE OF SCENERY. HE COULD
READ ME LIKE I READ MY PLANTS.

When my plants are barely drooping, I know just the right concoction
they need to offer a pick-me-up. When I begin to wilt, he's ready to
rehydrate me too, even before I know I need it myself. I extend my
plants a healthy gulp of their favorite, water. But Cory presented an
invitation to the place where internet is sparse and the moments are
easily touched; he knew the mountains were calling.

We live on the outskirts of Louisville, Kentucky, in a small country
city just a few handfuls of minutes east of the city's most eastern
suburb. The pace is slower here, but occasionally the city's tension can
be inhaled on our property if the wind blows in just the right direction. And in an always-connected world, it's hard to ever disconnect
entirely.

But just two hours farther east is the beginning of a glorious mountain range, and hidden within is a God-made natural bridge high in
the heavens always begging for foot traffic. The Red River Gorge was
a place others had often mentioned, but it wasn't until I was well into
my thirties that my husband surprised me with a secret birthday trip
to it.

I always thought I preferred the beach until I stepped foot in the
Gorge. And then I realized I just hadn't found my mountain yet.

Breaths are easier in the mountains, where the air is thin and prob-
lems seem distant. It is here I kayaked for the first time on top of a
dammed holler, paddling above old chimneys that had been flooded
with memories once and now were flooded literally. It's where you
can explore the depths of darkness in a clear-bottom kayak, and you
are so close to the water that you feel like you two are one. It's where
you get lost chasing a waterfall, and even if you don't find it, you

realize you find yourself in the process, and that's better anyway. At the Gorge, Mother Nature is your next-door neighbor, bringing deer to your doorstep and offering music in the air constantly as the birds sing and the wind tap dances among the trees.

THE FIRST TIME I STEPPED FOOT IN THIS HIDDEN TREASURE, I FELT AT HOME.

This trip felt like a family reunion where everyone brings a potluck dish to devour together while telling embarrassing memories on repeat.

The mountains were my extended family.
The trees were my distant second cousins.

I felt safe there, nestled in a log cabin in the woods. Some would be terrified by the silence that was ever so present, but not me. I was comforted by it.

Like a weighted blanket, it centered me easily, as if it had been calling my name to come rest in it.

We had packed some groceries, as Cory had some surprise meals concocted. And I had packed my computer and portable hotspot because I had some surprise plans too… to tackle Overwhelm head on and crank through some work between hikes. My husband knew better than to challenge me on that addition in our luggage because as a strong-willed gal, nothing was going to stop me.

Nothing that I could control at least.

When we arrived and got settled, I pulled out my portable office and plugged in all my equipment so I could occasionally stumble over to the screen and peck away at a project. But as the computer booted up,

I learned that no amount of will would encourage the trees to sway just enough for internet reception to be possible. I was in the middle of the mountains with no internet connection.

At first, Anxiety began having a heyday, excited to bubble up from my stomach and take residence in my throat. Overwhelm was also invited to that unexpected party for a bit, until Cory calmed my worries and reminded me that this getaway was meant to do just that. Get. Away. I decided to turn lemons into the sweetest lemonade I could find by using the time to write instead, a catharsis of mine I've utilized for much of my life.

After Cory warmed milk on the stove to blend with my chai tea and paired it with a tasty breakfast, I knew it was time. The mountain was calling. My feet were ready to respond. A hike was needed, and now was the time.

The July's heat was nearly unbearable, but we had plenty of frozen solid bottles of water ready and some granola bars in place for a mid-hike refuel. Cory's L.L.Bean backpack from his childhood was filled to the brim with everything we needed to hike to the Natural Bridge, a beautiful destination for hikers in our area.

The bridge is worth the work to get to it, but it's deceiving. No safety nets or guardrails ensure you remain on the seemingly thin bridge walkway countless feet in the air. And no barrier keeps the wind from gusting you off it. While not posing imminent danger, many heart-breaking cases of loss have occurred at the place we had our eyes set on.

For this height-fearing gal, the bridge is terrifying.
But the trek to get there posed its own difficulty too.

AS WITH ALL THINGS IN LIFE, THERE ARE SEVERAL PATHS THAT LEAD TO THE SAME DESTINATION.

Like a choose your own adventure story, the path you selected has its own hurdles and beauty. One took you around a beautiful running creek situated deep in the forest. Another offered a clearer path, one many families preferred. We had taken those before, so the new path we unearthed was calling; an adventure awaited.

It wasn't until we were too far on the path and turning back wasn't an option that we realized we had picked a trail destined to leave our knees wobbly and our breath behind. Ahead was an endless pathway of beautifully laid stepping stones. One by one, I coerced my legs to lift and step. Lift and step. The uneven nature of the rock and the land made for a challenge I definitely didn't sign up for but unexpectedly was forced to conquer.

Very few passersby broke up the monotonous hike, and I'm grateful for that being that in addition to my huffing and puffing, I'm confident that my deodorant was giving out. This gal that never sweats was sweating in places I didn't even know I had. There may not have been a running creek nearby, but my pores were working on overdrive to create one anyway. I pushed through waves of dizziness, and occasionally, I'd take the sound advice from Cory to stop, get a drink of the Arctic water found in his backpack and look around at God's artwork in our midst.

I would pause, take a gulp of water like my life depended upon it, and keep trudging ahead.

The pause was intentional, but I was also intentional about not letting my body enjoy too much of a break for fear it would prefer the break over the rest of the hike ahead.

The steps were so strenuous that I had little energy to sputter out any words, for that energy needed to be conserved to move my legs.

So, in lieu of inviting my husband into a deep conversation, I retreated within to find the one other person who always has my back (and this day, my legs): me. I could hear my heart beating in a rhythm like my body was making its own music to drown out the unwanted carry-ons that were always hiding in my midst: Anxiety and Over-whelm. The gentle and steady pulse of the blood flowing was like a yogic chant, drumming out the unnecessary so I could focus on the present. Like an unexpected instrument adding a grace note to an already beautiful piece of sheet music, my breaths were an equal contributor to the melody made for my ears alone.

When you become your song, you also become your lyrics. And the words of a pastor's recent story were quickly shaping into my chorus.

A FEW WEEKS PRIOR, WHILE AT CHURCH, OUR PASTOR SHARED A STORY THAT HAD ATTACHED ITSELF DEEP WITHIN ME WITHOUT PERMISSION.

I had forgotten about it entirely until my body began its chants, stirring it up within as if it was summoning it back into my consciousness for a reason only it and God knew.

The pastor told of a man who was preparing for his baptism. The man was a Navy SEAL, I believe, and had looked fear in the eye more than once. He had conquered what lived in many people's nightmares, and he came out on the other side a different person; a person who was ready to have an outward change reflective of the inner work he had experienced. Right before his baptism, however, he had made a request of the pastor that was a bit out of character.

"When you baptize me," he asked, "will you hold me down for several minutes?"

Even though this man had lungs of steel and had no fear of drowning, the pastor was extremely uncomfortable abiding by his wishes (for obvious reasons of course). "Why?" was his reply.

"Why would you want to be held under for that amount of time?" A logical question to an illogical request. The man's response was a gut punch. "I have a lot to leave in the water," he said.

Don't we all? On repeat, I kept hearing what the man said like my melody had become a broken record. Life was hard. The world was tough. Worries had been storming in and uncertainty was hiding behind each tree I passed by. While optimism had always been my bestie, rough patches find everyone no matter the amount of perspective you carry in your backpack.

As the sweat poured from my face and my legs were making Jell-O for the unrequested potluck meal my forest family was hosting, Cory offered a momentary reprieve again. With all the water I was losing, I needed to replenish my body with more to stay hydrated. But I wasn't ready to stop. There was power in movement. There was a calmness my body was creating and the forest had offered with the trees, shading me from all my "stuff." The harder I walked, the louder the music. But I couldn't drown out the message the moment was offering. It was then that I understood.

I stopped once I found a flat rock, and with tears streaming down my face, I gazed at my husband with a look that offered our souls to talk to one another and told him what I had just uncovered. "I have a lot to leave in the water too," I shared. "But my water is here. In the forest. On hikes. With the trees. I have a lot to leave here. Can the forest hold me under for a few more minutes?"

The trees hear without me ever speaking a word.
They offer a peace I couldn't find elsewhere.
God is easier to find when you step foot in his sanctuary.

He commanded each of these trees to grow just like he commanded the waters to gather and separate from the heavens. His Will will always be done, and all I have to do is surrender to it and embrace the relief it offers. No burden needs to be carried alone. It's too heavy to do so, and he doesn't want that for you or for me. Alongside each step up that mountain, God was there as my cheerleader and as my walking stick, offering balance and support each and every step.

I DIDN'T GO TO MILITARY TRAINING. I DEFINITELY DON'T HAVE LUNGS OF STEEL.

Instead of being baptized in water that day, I poured the water from within out. While I don't know all that the Navy SEAL needed to leave in the water, I did understand the breakthrough that the water offered him. It was offered to me too. And it's readily accessible for you as well.

That day, we made it to the top of the Natural Bridge where, with my eyes closed, my husband guided me across the most beautiful piece of scenery my stomach wasn't ready for this height-fearing girl to gaze upon just yet. And while my breaths steadied at the top of the mountain, I realized triumph wasn't found when we crossed the finish line, stepping foot on our destination.

Instead, the end wasn't ever the destination. The middle was, and my success was found there, in the forest, where the trees remained steady when I wasn't. The middle was messy as the path wasn't straight and each step uneven.

The middle was both the problem and the solution.
It was both the teacher and the student.

It was where I was gifted a multitude of minutes under water where I could leave my worries behind and make it to the other side a different person altogether.

I now know that I can't outrun Overwhelm and Anxiety, but I can outwit them when I run to the mountains.

There they don't have the stamina to make the trek up the steep inclines. They want you to get lost in them, not lost in God's space. There in the mountains they aren't welcome, and they know it.

Breakthroughs are possible when you listen to the music of your soul and God's lyrics written for you and to you. For me, I hear them best in the mountains.

The Conditions

❦

There is truly nothing better than a crisp spring breeze, the subtle smell of fresh air intermingling with the sun's rays and the annoying yet satisfying feeling of having God's rich earth covering the crevices of your hands, deep into your fingerprints and farther down your nails than you knew possible.

The only thing I can think of to top off that deliciousness is a meal derived from the goodness found from something you've nurtured to grow.

When life gets chaotic, I turn to the dirt. I always have and always will because gardening is in my genetics.

As a youngun with my overnight bag packed, I hopped in my dad's blue pickup truck with my cousin in tow, and together we met up with my grandparents on their farm for a weekend of manual labor and countless memories.

WHEN THEY FIRST BOUGHT THE FARM, IT WAS MERELY ACRES OF POSSIBILITY.

As the years went on, I was able to watch it grow as my family built an outhouse (the best and cleanest one in the country, thanks to my grandma who ensured that it was just as fancy as going to a five-star hotel would be). They built a barn by hand and dug a pond while expanding the original one that came with the property.

Cattle joined our family—several of which acted more like domesticated dogs—as did a horse for a brief moment. But my favorite part of the farm was always the garden.

You always knew dinner would be delicious when Grandma cooked a farm-grown meal of wilted lettuce and a crisp tomato and onion salad covered in vinegar, pepper and more sugar than I cared to measure. There was nothing quite like raw radishes or the first bite of marbled sweet corn straight off the cob that we had just picked hours earlier.

Food I wouldn't dare try at home was fair game here, where everything tasted a bit differently, likely from the TLC that was added into the fertilizer.

I learned so much on that farm, such as the value of hard work and commitment. Dad built me a treehouse with those two soft skills. I learned the importance of perseverance and how that is easily coupled with a level of exhaustion you never knew possible. Nightly, as we would congregate around a bonfire my grandma took pleasure in poking, you could see a level of tiredness that you don't find elsewhere.

Most of all I learned the power of patience and how the taste of patience is worth everything.

THE FIRST PLACE I CALLED MY OWN HOME AS A YOUNG ADULT WAS A TINY CONDO THAT WAS PART OF A POORLY RENOVATED ELDERLY HOME.

It came complete with non-working "help me, I can't get up" drawstrings in each room and the smallest patch of soil for this gardener to utilize. It was pathetic to say the least, but I used every inch of it to plant a few tomato plants. My garden expanded when my husband and I bought our first home, but my heart grew tenfold when we found the perfect slice of heaven nestled in the outer reach of the city we grew up in to expand even more. Another twenty-five acres awaited—this time requiring me to take lead—for more memories, more togetherness and, what I came to learn, more patience.

We weren't fully settling into our farm life when the world caved in. The pandemic caused everyone and everything to be a bit out of sorts, unsure of what was real, what was really coming and what to do about either. As true to my nature, when uncertainty lingers, I go where I'm comfortable, and before stores closed for the unforeseeable future and fear enveloped all, I found myself in the local home improvement store collecting everything I could to grow my own vegetable starters.

I had made friends with a local farmer who found much joy in germinating seeds to offer gardeners like me a leg up in the vegetable plant process.

"Starters," as they are called, give you the best chance for success. The hard part is really done. The seeds have been loved on and nourished. The seedlings had been hardened off, and they were always ready for any harsh conditions a Kentucky summer could and would throw at them. But I was terrified that my trusted starter supplier wouldn't have any plants for me due to the pandemic, and time would go wasted as I prepared for my homesteading.

I bought more seeds than one could plant in a decade and as many grow lights as the store had in stock. I looked like I knew what I was doing, but I was as clueless as anyone. I knew enough to be dangerous when it came to reading a seed packet. And I had heard grow lights offered something natural light didn't always give. Outside of that and high hopes, I was totally and completely in the dark (or I guess, since I bought nearly twenty grow lights, I would soon be more in the light than not).

My office would become my indoor habitat prepared precisely for over two-hundred seeds of potential.

At any given time, when stress would wash over me, I could be found in this space planting, watering and watching. Great things began and quickly. I looked forward to waking up and heading to work where I was in good company with a few hundred of my babies. Many grew several inches and leaves of all shapes and sizes took form.

Growth is so fun to watch.
The opposite, however, is heart-breaking to endure.

THAT MORNING WAS LIKE MOST.

I woke up, grateful to live outside of city limits where we could mentally pretend that change wasn't happening around us, and after a shower and breakfast, I was ready to check in on my babies. When I opened the door, however, I was devastated. Overnight, a plague of some sort wiped out each and every one. Hundreds of new growth and boundless potential were nothing more than soil. For you are dust, and to dust you shall return, I guess.

I was a puddle. And that was just the beginning of my gardening saga that year. My starter supplier indeed, praise the good Lord, had not let the pandemic halt his efforts. However, the first round of starters that I bought from him to plant in our massive garden were killed by a late and unexpected frost. The second round we planted was ruined by a massive windstorm. And the final round we mustered up the strength to put in never took root because the soil hadn't been properly fertilized.

After four attempts, I folded, giving up on my favorite pastime and neglected the space that always brought me joy. Weeds overtook the newly created garden, and I couldn't even bear to look at the eyesore in our backyard.

That is, until the following year when a friend reignited my gardening flame. At the first taste of an approaching spring, she shared her approach for growing seedlings, and I decided I'd give it a shot. Surely, I told myself, I had learned from my mishaps.

However, I was quickly stressed to the max. Her approach was completely different from what I had tackled before. I was used to growing lights and soil as the basis of germination. She suggested a concoction of wet paper towels, Ziploc baggies and whatever seeds I wanted to try. She created mini greenhouses to encourage seed growth, and I was quickly out of my gardening league. She offered no guidebook, and outside of the supportive texts and insights from her learned experience, all I had to go on was faith and hope alone.

One day, after I reached out to her, panicking that I was surely ruining another round of seeds, she offered me some sound life advice (and gardening advice too).

"Girl, don't stress!" she said. "Remember, seeds *want* to grow. Just give them a little water and sunshine."

It was a lightbulb moment for sure and one that has sat with me for years since. A seed doesn't want to stay dormant. It wasn't created to.

It was designed for growth, always. Its dormant state is meant to protect it, not hold it back. The seed would prefer to not remain a seed forever. It really wants to grow. All it asks for to make it happen is the right conditions.

WHETHER YOU ARE A GARDENER OF VEGETABLES OR SEEKING TO GARDEN YOUR OWN LIFE, HER WORDS OF WISDOM RING TRUE FOR US ALL.

The seeds we carry—whether they are as tiny as a pinpoint or as large as a melon—*want* action taken. They want growth.

They don't seek to stay dormant for years. They don't want to be forgotten in the kitchen junk drawer. They were designed to bring forth new life of various kinds.

They have a purpose—in the soil of a backyard garden and the soil of our souls—to inspire growth and be the catalyst for it. They don't want to stay small forever; they want to help each of us grow to our fullest potential. All they need is some nourishment, adequate light and someone who is willing to help connect the two and give them a fighting chance.

The Clover

Few things bring me as much joy as witnessing my children erupt into deep, uncontrollable laughter. In that moment, it's clear they are carefree, and my heart swells to its fullest. Providing unexpected assistance to someone else fills me with a sense of completeness and goodness. Such acts of kindness offer me a glimpse into the true meaning of life, and the ensuing sense of inner peace is indescribable. Just like walking in a greenhouse filled with as many flowers as humidity. There, life is abundant, and all are thankful for deodorant.

Each of these costs nothing and brings more happiness than anything money could buy. When all three collide, my joy nearly explodes.

When the family and I laugh in our garden, dodging the tomato bugs while collecting each and every cherry tomato ready to add to our dinner's salad, I feel full. It's like a complete circle; one that just makes me smile with a deep level of contentment.

SO, AS ONE COULD IMAGINE, WHEN OUR GARDEN
EXPERIENCED A DROUGHT, I FELT IT TOO.

The first year of any garden adventure always leaves more to be
desired. The soil isn't perfected yet, and the dirt Dad hauled in, we
found out later, wasn't nutrient-rich top soil. We had acres upon acres
of land, but year after year, our harvest left much to be desired, and I
was beyond disappointed.

"Why did you buy a farm?" many people asked.
"What animals are on your farm?" they followed up with.

Great questions, and yet my consistent remark outlined my vision for
a massive garden; one where others could come enjoy and I could
teach the kids how to live off the land. Envisioning this dream filled
my soul; executing it did quite the opposite.

The year prior, not only did I kill each and every vegetable starter
I grew from seed, but the starters that I purchased to plant in the
garden died, three times over.

The frost, the wind and the poor soil ruined each batch. We gave up,
and boycotted buying anything from farmer's markets just because.

That year, the seeds I sprouted had promise. I had purchased a small,
portable greenhouse at the advice of a friend, but I hadn't considered
that our home perched on one of the highest parts of the city, where
the wind was always extreme. Twice, the greenhouse blew away and
took each beautiful seed of possibility with it. I was no longer disappointed, I was embarrassed and frustrated.

If you weren't into gardening, you may have suggested I throw in the
towel and invest in a crop-share program. Give in and support
another local farmer who has more of a green thumb, you'd tell me.

That's sound advice, I'll give you that. But much like a vocation isn't something you choose, being a gardener—for me—is a part of my identity. Even if I wanted to toss in the towel, my body wouldn't let me. It would still find a way to pull on my rain boots and put on the gardening gloves to plant something, even if it was destined for failure.

BUT FAILURE ISN'T AN OPTION. IT NEVER HAS BEEN, AND IT WASN'T GOING TO BE THEN EITHER.

So, instead, I chose another path, one where I planned to learn from my mishaps.

Why, oh why, didn't the garden produce anything previously?
Why did my starter plants shrivel?
Why wasn't any of it easy?

I had many questions, and in searching for larger answers, I made small, incremental changes and then persistently watched, knowing the answer would reveal itself soon.

As with most things in life, I was deep in a cycle—make a change, watch the outcome, adapt accordingly. Whether you are hands deep in a garden or attempting to tackle a challenge at work, that cycle can show promise everywhere and anywhere. And that year, when I went out to the garden, I was reminded that not only does that cycle help you move forward, but it also provides you with new opportunities.

It had been a long day, and a longer night awaited. The candle was being burned at both ends, but the garden was calling. When you live on a farm, the work is never done, and while I knew I didn't have time to dig in, I knew I needed to visit it. I put on my rain boots covered in a colorful kitty-cat pattern and began my trek to the overgrowth that was once my garden.

Green sprouted from every angle, and yet, not a single vegetable plant had been planted. Ever wondered why you can't get a beautiful flower to grow in your landscape, but dandelions have no trouble at all making it their permanent residence? The same situation held true for my garden.

The soil had been so desolate that it looked like cracked desert terrain; that is until we covered it in cow manure.

Years ago, when my family and I lived in our old house with a mature garden we had nurtured for a decade, people would ask me what our tips were for reaping such a plentiful variety of all fruits and vegetables and my answer was a simple one.

While I wanted to sing the childhood nursery rhyme, I had a different ending to offer.

Mary, Mary, quite contrary, How does your garden grow?
With silver bells and cockleshells and pretty maids all in a row.
No, really it's thanks to the manure.

When the garden had given its all for the year, we would burn the remaining sprigs of leaves and then cover the space with manure, letting it soak into the depths of the soil for months before asking it again to help provide nourishment for our family. Gross, right?! Who wants to smell manure, much less toss it around to cover the entire garden?

The first year we did it, I'm not going to lie, I was a bit sickened by it all, but seeing the benefits made me a believer. And the more I learned and perfected my gardening, the more I realized how important this step was.

Letting the soil rest is critical; but letting it rest and rejuvenate is pure brilliance. It's like a spa day for the garden; but the facial lasts much longer, and there isn't a need for anything more than an annual mud wrap.

The plants suck the soil dry, and covering the soil in manure—kind of like covering us in a blanket at night—gives it energy while renewing the nutrients needed for another year of a bountiful garden.

MY GARDEN HAD BEEN SMOTHERED IN A THICK BLANKET OF COW MANURE.

And its winter warmth was growing green clover everywhere. In fact, the grass on the garden looked better than the grass on the yard, interestingly enough. While I stood there, soaking in the truth that in a few days, the garden would be home to new plants full of potential and saying a silent prayer that maybe this year would be our year, I looked down and saw a glimpse of hope.

There, standing up strong and proud, in the thick of the manure-grown clover was a five-leaf beauty. I'd never seen one before and was sure it was an optical illusion trying to trick me.

But as I bent down and plucked the weed, I saw its perfection. It was, indeed, an anomaly. And in the sea of dense clover, I knew that it was a matter of divine intervention that I found this one. It was placed there for me as a reminder of the power that I will always hold.

Some of my best inspirations in life come from my sweet, little garden in the backyard hills of Kentucky. The stories it's heard of mine and the tears it has wiped away for me have been endless. And the life lessons it's taught me have been game changing.

That moment, as I plucked up the five-leaf clover, I knew that even when my life feels covered in challenge, disappointment and disgust—

times when I feel like I am covered in manure—I am merely being gifted a moment of rest so that I can soak in the energy and goodness I need for the next season in life.

During those times, I get to choose what I do with the weeds I may see around me. And you do as well.

You can allow the clover to take over, like my garden had attempted to do, not creating any space for new planting. Or you can realize that the clover has purpose too, and instead, stand proud and reach up, realizing that life isn't about luck but rather choice; choice in how you see the world, how you see your circumstances and how you see yourself.

You can try to make lemonade out of lemons any day, but next time life hands you a pile of manure, opt to grow a five-leaf clover instead.

The Save

Most moments of your life are forgotten, tossed away in a well never to be recollected again, no matter the amount of will you set forth. There are moments you wish you could uncover, like the penny hiding deep within. But most are perfectly comfortable far away from your memory.

They shaped you but don't own you. They are gone for a reason.

But other moments you want to shake and can't. They hold onto you with such vigor, as if they have something more to teach you before they can detach. It feels like their grip will forever be tight. Some of those moments are poignant. The moments of my grandparents' last breaths are some. The moments of when I said, "I do" and when my husband and I welcomed our kids into this world. Those moments I'll cherish forever, hoping they never leave my memory.

Others, though, I wish I could break free from.
One of those is the day that I almost lost my littlest.

WHEN WE BOUGHT THE FARM, IT WAS AS IF WE COULDN'T BREATHE UNLESS WE WERE TRAVERSING IT.

There was no bathroom... no house... no shed or garden. It was just rolling land complete with two subpar ponds and a running creek hidden in the woods at the back of the property. Life changed the moment we would pull up to our slice of heaven and unpack our crew, a picnic and as many tools as our van could safely carry. We had plans. We had land. But we hadn't a clue how to connect the two.

While we attempted to figure out where the garden would become a permanent fixture and where the orchard would be set up, we held bonfires with friends.

With their kids in tow, the land became a place for community, complete with sticky fingers from roasted marshmallows, the crackling of cedar wood and plenty of exploring for all ages. We loved how the land brought people together instead of dividing them based on differences.

Land has a way of beautifully doing that. Water, on the other hand, has the potential for the complete opposite.

It was seasonably cold on the day where this moment will forever live. Everyone came bundled with knitted scarfs and cotton gloves, oversized hats and puff jackets filled with down feathers. The wind was dulled enough so as to not rub it in your face that the cold could overtake you if it wanted to. Without that in place, the bonfire would never have happened that day. When you stood still, you could manage the frigid temperature. And the warmth from the fire was a welcomed addition to all.

It was customary for my husband and I to separate during these bonfires, wearing differing hospitality hats so as to ensure each of our friends and their families felt as welcomed on our land as our land offered to us. He was cooking hotdogs over the fire while I opted to take a group of ten or so parents and kiddos to the creek, which was a bit of a hike and not one for the weary. To get to the creek required a trek down a hill that was really meant to be used for the dropout of a roller coaster. Its incline was strong and after the recent rain, it was also quite muddy and slippery. Hiking boots were a must, and most in attendance weren't sporting them, my son included.

LUKE WAS JUST A LITTLE GUY THEN. MAYBE THREE OR FOUR.

He hadn't become calloused to the world just yet, and his appetite for adventure always was more intense than his desire for safety. I knew this, and I became accustomed to growing a pair of eyes in the back of my head because of it. "Where's Luke?" was as common of a phrase that slipped through my lips as "Good morning."

We made it to the creek in one piece as a collective unit of parents with delighted children who saw a vast playground with no end as a treasure map for new beginnings. Many hadn't seen our creek before and stood in awe of the peace that the steady flow of water offered.

Peace does indeed flow like a river, until you remember that the river doesn't stop for the weary or for the child. Instead, it continues whether you are ready for it or not.

Most kids hopped from stone to stone to one side of the creek and back. Others tossed rocks into the creek, hoping to skip them like their parents were doing. The depth of the creek on our property was shallow—less than a foot or so at its deepest parts—which was its usual state. But right over the property line was a danger zone, and one that I had made clear to all around that you didn't want to explore.

The creek on our property is always moving. But it is as if the moment it flows under the low-lying fencing meant to define our property line, the water stops. There it collects. Branches create dams and nothing moves. In fact, I have always felt like it does quite the opposite there… it dies. Stagnant water draws mosquitoes and snakes, both of which would be the last things I would want to see while enjoying the bubbling creek of peace. Stagnant water collects dirt and invites algae. What was once clean just feels downright gross.

My family always opted to play on our property, and with over twenty-five acres to explore, there was always enough. But my little Luke has always been the one to push beyond life's edges.

Don't tell him he can't do something because when you do, it's the first thing he'll try. While the other kids were stone hopping, Luke got too close for comfort to the stagnant water hole, and I made every attempt to encourage him and his rubber boots to explore the water farther away from the lifeless abyss.

I'LL NEVER KNOW WHAT WAS IN HIS HEAD THAT DAY.

I don't know if he was attempting to not fall out of his oversized waterproof boots as he pivoted toward the left, where the creek was full of life. Or was he exploring the unknown, taking a peek into the dark waterhole that always gave me the heebee jeebees? Either way, a mere moment—a second—changed everything.

The rock he was hopping on was as slippery as the ground we had hiked down. His foot went one way and his body the other, and as I watched in slow motion, with him out of arm's reach, he fell into the stagnant water. It enveloped him as if it was waiting for its prey, and it had been hungry for a while. My mind didn't move as fast as my heart pounded. Instead, it paused for a moment with assurance that he would stand up in the water no deeper than my knees, and we'd have a wet Luke on our hands as the only side effect.

But that isn't what happened.

Instead, Luke began rolling like lumberjacks roll logs down large rivers. As he rolled up for breath and back under the water, his eyes rolled too, as if his body was fighting to determine who would win this battle.

Surely he's going to stand up, I thought. Surely.

But he didn't. His lifeless body rolled maybe two times over before my legs moved my body to him.

I had no thoughts as fear took over every cell in my body. Fear became my catalyst to save my little boy.

The water was ice cold, and each layer of my clothing, originally intended to keep my body warm, added unintentional weight. My soul was heavy and my body too. I was only a few steps away from him, but it felt like eternity to reach where he was fighting for his life.

I fell on my way, realizing that part of his struggle wasn't what was happening above the water; instead it was below. Later I would define it as quicksand; the earth swallowing me under as I tried to be the lifeline for one of the three beating hearts outside of my own.

I grabbed Luke with as much strength as I could muster, but the unexpected weight of my jeans and layered jacket paired with the deadweight of his body and winter clothing was too much for my arms to hold alone. With every ounce of strength I had, I tried to lift him. But as I did, the creek bed laughed, pulling me in. The algae-covered stones hidden under the murky water also offered no reprieve.

FOR EVERY ATTEMPT I HAD TO SAVE MY SON, I FOUND MYSELF MAKING MATTERS WORSE.

I would lift him up for a momentary glimpse of hope. Then I would fall back on top of him, unintentionally pushing his body deeper into the shallow waters.

Fear paused for a moment, offering my conscious thoughts to appear. It was then that I realized not only was Luke drowning, but I was too. In my efforts to save him, we were both dying. Together.

Between the gulps of dirty creek water, where my yells were muffled and silenced, I would use the brief opportunities for breath to scream a simple word, but the one that saved us both.

Help!

I learned later that the scene from the bystanders appeared much different than what was happening to the two of us in the water. We were fighting to live. But our friends saw what appeared to be a playful splashing. Surely Stephanie could just stand up in the waterbed and all would be well, our friends told me later they thought. The severity of the situation wasn't visible to the naked eye, only to the eyes struggling to see the light.

One of the dads heard my cry for help and came running. He grabbed us both by our jackets and pulled us to safety, just a few feet from what could have been our deathbed. Others began asking if I was alright, but I cared nothing for me, only my son. I stared at Luke with such force as the other parents began to determine if he needed CPR.

Water spewed from his mouth after a few coughs, and outside of a perpetual shake from the frigid temps and creek-soaked clothing,

Luke left the creek the same healthy boy he had arrived as. I, on the other hand, became forever changed.

WATER IS A NECESSITY FOR OUR GROWTH AND NOURISHMENT.

It offers a reprieve to the summer's heat. It's a welcomed soother in the middle of the night, the storms calming a weary soul's worries. It is pure. It offers cleansing and rebirth. It's one of the few things both us and the rest of the earth's living things need to survive.

When it's moving, it's life giving.
But it can also be life taking.

Years prior to this moment, I had a run-in with its might during an unexpected and terrifying whitewater rafting mishap. I remember the currents pulling me under and looking up through the stained-glass pieces of the water's churn, begging God to pull me out for a much-needed deep breath of air.

I learned to respect water then. And I was reminded of that during this moment as well.

The water followed us back to the campfire in the soles of my shoes. As I sloshed and shivered, I prayed a continual prayer of gratitude. But equally fighting for my attention over and over in my head was a slow-motion movie stuck on repeat. Between my prayers played the story of what could have happened in the moments.

The what-ifs overrode the what-didn'ts.
Fear wouldn't let up its grip.

Friends gave Luke new clothes to wear, complete with pink flowers and several sizes too big. But we were grateful. He was warm. I stood by the campfire, no longer relaxed. Instead, every nerve ending was tightened, creating knots in my stomach and my back alike. My body wept in hopes to center my soul and rid it of the water that almost took us. But I couldn't shake the experience.

The few words I muttered were a replay of what could have happened. It was as if I was convincing myself that it did until another set of parents embraced me, grounded me back to the moment, and reminded me of the truth. What could have happened didn't. And I had a sweet little boy running around, happy as could be, as a reminder of it.

THE CONDITIONS FOR GROWTH ARE THE SAME CONDITIONS FOR LOSS.

Soil offers nutrients for a seed to break free, and it is what is tossed over our casket when our life here is complete. The sun offers us warmth, but it was the Son's ultimate sacrifice that paid the price for us. And water, a necessity to sustain us, can easily rob us of our future if we aren't carefully watching.

The same is true for saving. I thought I could save my Luke, only to find that I made matters worse.

Saving isn't something that can be done alone or in a silo. Without our friends congregating around the water pit, there would have been a different outcome to our story.

I could let that moment be the moment on replay forever and always, knowing that it has turned into a core memory that would have a grip on me for the rest of my living days.

Or I could change that, and instead see that moment as a reminder that breakthroughs happen when we find a momentary gulp of air and make a choice to use it for the betterment of everyone, not just ourselves. That gulp could have given me the ammunition to hold my breath longer while underneath the water's surface. That could have worked. But instead, I took a risk. I took a chance to speak instead of taking the much-needed breath my body ached for. A cry for help was all it took for someone to arrive and save us that moment.

A small slip can pull you into a puddle of quicksand. An offer to help another could pull you down with them. But a cry for help can be the gift you give another to take over and pull you to safety. Together.

Breakthroughs aren't accomplished alone. Sometimes you offer the life vest and other times you need it.

Either way, no matter the water's depth or your skills for doggie paddling, the way to make it to the water's edge and safe grounds is by surrendering the belief that you can be the savior. You may be able to create the *break*, but the *through*? That requires the healing hand of another and a moment that connects the two.

PART FOUR

The Growth

Every seasoned gardener has a toolkit. Packed within it are everyday tools required to care for their seedlings, encouraging and supporting their growth.

You'll find a garden spade and a dandelion weeder.
Cloth gloves create a needed barrier between thorny weeds and pests.
Garden kneelers support knees when you are supporting plants.
Watering cans direct water where plants need it most, the roots.

A gardener of life, too, has a toolkit, complete with necessities to facilitate personal growth as well. However, these tools don't fit in a backpack or gardening basket.

While proper nourishment and fresh water are important, sufficient rest, purposeful breaths, adequate time and a healthy dose of faith offer a deeper level of sustenance for the soul.

Just as a garden needs time, care and attention to flourish, so do we.

The Green Thumb

~ ~ ~

It's quiet on Saturday mornings. There's no eager hustle to brush teeth and scarf mini pancakes in hopes to fill a tummy and fuel a brain for a day of learning. The low hum of the heater flows as I become the first to walk around the house exploring our nocturnal zoo of cats with the lights off and the pitch black enveloping me like a warm and cozy hug.

I can breathe deeper when the quiet is paired with the darkness. The rest of my family doesn't understand my love for shuffling in the dark, dodging cat landmines and backpacks while navigating to my hidden escape above the garage where I write and work and ponder. But I love this me time where the only ones awake are those who talk without speaking a word.

It's just me.
Our cats.
And the plants.

By no means am I a hoarder; in fact, I'm quite the opposite. If it hasn't been used frequently, it's out and pronto. For years we had a closet that we prayed no one would open for fear of their life as all the leftovers, unwanteds and forgottens lived there waiting for a spare moment of mine to sell in an online yard sale group. Until one day, I had had enough and packed it all in bags for charity. That day I gave up my passion to hoard kid toys to one day sell and rested in the truth that, instead, I'll just hoard plants.

I REMEMBER MY GRANDMA'S HUMBLE APARTMENT LIKE I VISITED IT JUST YESTERDAY, ALTHOUGH IT'S BEEN OVER A DECADE NOW SINCE SHE LAST OCCUPIED IT.

Her space was filled with collectables from yard sales, but another's trash was absolutely her treasure. And anything in her space were my treasures too. She was my cheerleader, and I forever will be hers.

She had a glass bowl perched on the end table nestled tightly by her prized possession, a couch my mom gifted her worth more than every item in her house combined. That bowl was a mini candy shop filled to the brim with bite-sized delights.

Above her fridge was a snowman ceramic that was a year-round fixture. The hat lifted off to unveil a sea of pennies. I never knew or even asked where they all came from, but the moment I stepped foot into her safe haven, I could hear the unsnapping of a Ziploc bag and the clinking of handfuls of copper coins filling it. I never left without a bag to fill my penny jar with too.

Grandma's candy bowl is proudly seated on our bookshelves where I can sense her presence daily as our family joins together to watch the newest show on Netflix. Just this past Christmas, my mom gifted me Grandma's snowman, which now holds our cutlery captive on the kitchen counter. My youngest occasionally—and without my knowing—recreates the familiar sound of collected coins as he offers his found treasures into the ceramic beauty for safe keeping. And while I'm grateful for these two invaluable pieces of memory, what I'm more grateful for is the green thumb my grandma passed on to my generation.

When you walked into Grandma's apartment, you could almost hear the plants singing joyous songs of gratitude as she would nurture them like she did me.

I don't remember what color her walls were painted, but I remember her place feeling green to the brim. Next to the one of only two windows her place had was more plants than one woman should ever own. She was proud of each, and they sported the confidence that anyone would have if someone believed in them an ounce of what she did in her plant friends.

It was in this small apartment I learned that the secret sauce to making a philodendron sparkle was using mayonnaise to clean its leaves of dust. It was in this space that I anxiously anticipated the annual welcoming of color when Christmas or Easter would appear alongside the cactuses that only bloomed that time of year with consistency. Until then, the space was green. But then, it was full of color.

GRANDMA LOVED HER PLANTS, AND I DO MINE.

The only difference was she didn't have to barter with the feline family members to preserve the life of each, and the plant growing process came as naturally to her as seeing people where they are and loving them all the same. She would talk to her plant babies like she talked to me, with ease and all her heart. "They hear you," she would tell me. "And they are encouraged by your words."

Saturdays are watering days in our household. I've slowly collected a dozen or two of living, breathing greenery in our home that beg for nourishment these mornings. Some days, I water in the darkness, where I can whisper sweet nothings to a life that many overlook. Other days, I invite my kids to partake in the fun. My daughter gets a pep in her step when I ask her to fill up the measuring cup, our vessel for watering. My youngest son, on the other hand, just shakes his head.

One morning, he showed interest, so I pulled out two measuring cups —the four-cup version for me and the little one for him. Together, we walked through our living space, spotting each plant and offering it breakfast.

As we watered each, I would pause, look at the plant and try to cypher what it was trying to communicate to me.

One had some yellow leaves. I touched the soil, which was still damp, and opted to give it another week before rehydrating him.

Another was getting leggy as it leaned to one side, an indication of where the sun was most present as he was reaching for it. To offer the stem strength, I told my little Luke, you need to turn the pot occasionally, so the lean isn't so lopsided.

The last looked sad. Its drooping leaves told me that it didn't like its current home and was asking for a new place to try out. It didn't have legs to move itself, but I could and I did, offering it a new resting place as I promised I would check in on it in the coming days to see what it thought.

As I spoke to each, my son's eyebrows would burrow deeper with thought. It wasn't until we were nearly complete that he said what must have been on his mind the whole time. "Momma," he stated and followed up with such matter-of-factness. "Why do you care so much for these plants? You do know they are just a piece of grass." He continued to lecture me on the fact that it made no sense for us to have what God intended to be outside of our home inside and at such a quantity.

HIS BRAIN IS SOMETHING SPECIAL TO WATCH WORK.

At a ripe age of seven, you can see him piece together, bit-by-bit, all the knowledge that has been poured into him to create a solution to a problem he uncovers. It's quite remarkable to observe and humorous, at times, to see what he concludes. That day I learned of what he really thought of my plant collection: unnecessary.

What I saw as life-giving growth, he saw as a near-distant cousin of the grass blade that populated our farm. What I saw as beautiful decor, he saw as a waste of time, energy and water.

From the outside looking in, I can appreciate how senseless my plant talking appeared to the naked eye. An opportunity was at hand, and I opted to invite him into the conversation. While grass and plants look the same in many ways, I definitely don't believe that I have grass planted throughout my home. Instead, each plant has a personality independent of the rest, and I wanted to introduce Luke to each.

I took him, first, to the plants recovering in our bedroom. These three had been through the wringer. They were not thriving in other spaces, and I feared placing them in our bedroom would be a welcomed invitation for our cats to enjoy an unhealthy afternoon snack outside of my watch. But when you are on the brink of giving up, you're willing to try anything with a glimmer of hope.

I explained to Luke how two of the three plants were actually family members. Years ago I had purchased a pilea plant when they were still new to the US. I was enthralled by their space-like leaves and loved learning that they propagate from the root up. Once the plant is comfortable and happy, they will birth babies all around them, miniature versions of their strong and healthy parent. This one plant had produced over a dozen babies I had sold or gifted to others and many that we have hidden around the home. But her leaves had begun to fail her, and I took the risk of cutting her off at the stem and attempting to generate roots from it in open water. It was a big risk, but it came with a bigger reward. She wasn't just surviving; she was thriving, and so was her relative. Happily, they had found their forever home.

I next took Luke to one of my favorite stubborn plants, the African violet. My grandma's apartment was filled with oodles of these beauties so, naturally, it was one that I was determined to have in my home. As I repotted her, I could hear my grandma whispering in my ear the hidden truth of this variety. Its leaves are enticing to touch. Their velvety nature, however, can't handle the oils from our fingertips and will wither if we override its request to be only looked at, not touched. Water must be offered at the base, too, not to come in contact with its leaves. And only when she is comfortable will she offer up a bloom that will surprise and delight.

Three years of life in our home and I was still waiting for a bloom. I was determined, however, to not give up hope.

Confident that sharing the plants' stories with Luke would open his eyes to their beauty, I asked what he thought, assured he would redirect his previous statement to one of deeper understanding. "It's just grass, Momma," was his answer, and he went off to play Legos instead.

A smirk was painted on my face and a giggle hidden within it. His eyes were still maturing, and his knowledge still evolving. It took me years to understand the love Grandma had for her plants. It would likely take years for him to see it too. And that was beyond okay.

ONE DAY, HE WILL DISCOVER HOW WE AREN'T SO DIFFERENT FROM OUR PLANT FRIENDS. IN FACT, THEY TEACH US MORE THAN WE COULD EVER DO FOR THEM, I'M CERTAIN.

Just because they don't speak, they still talk. Their language is different than ours but equally as important. We don't have to understand them to love them. And at the core of every living being is a yearn to be loved and cared for, to be understood without having to understand.

Just because they don't visibly move, they grow. Their movement is methodical, and their growth is always up, toward the warmth the sun offers. They don't need full sunlight; in fact, some varieties would shrivel up from it. But the sun can make its way through the twists and turns of hallways and find whatever is seeking its presence. God's Son does the same.

Just because they can't help out with the dishes doesn't mean they don't contribute. They absolutely do. They help purify the air and bring still-ness to our hearts. They are a constant reminder of the cornerstones of a healthy life by offering us a heaping reminder that the words we say matter, so we should choose them wisely. And many times we speak without ever saying a word. Our actions, in fact, may matter more.

There are as many houseplant varieties as people who walk this earth, I am sure. Each with a unique difference but equally as important.

The small can be mighty, and the large can get weary. The stubborn are likely just cautious, awaiting the comfort to show their true colors. But many just want to be loved at the depths that my grandma loved her plants. They want to be turned ever so slightly so as to be given a little push in the right direction. They want someone to notice when they could use a pick-me-up. They want to be seen and not overlooked.

A green thumb implies that I am the one in charge of the plant's growth potential. But the green thumb I inherited, I believe, holds a different meaning. Instead, it's the eyes-wide-open kind of love where you create the conditions for growth to happen and the encouragement to offer a loving push in the right direction.

The Toolkit

~~~

The short breaths commenced, and through them heat rose up my neck. It felt as though time stopped while I tried to break free of the nonexistent but completely real feeling of suffocation. The duration of each episode was as unknown, as was when one would resurface again, and the more they frequented, the tougher it was becoming to dislodge from them.

Panic. Anxiety. Worry. If you're among the lucky who can conquer life without one of these words wiggling in, I envy you. For me, they have always followed me, showing up at a young age when I would fret over an upcoming test in school (yes, I was that kid). They have made themselves evident when deadlines hovered, and they always like showing up just when I think I've got my life together, only to remind me that as together I feel, I will always need God to be my glue.

While their occurrence is unpredictable, one thing is certain: I've found that if I can bring with me the tools I've collected over the years, I can better manage their arrival.

NO AMOUNT OF RAINBOW WISHING WILL REMOVE ALL THUNDERSTORMS.

While I'd love to only delight in butterflies, the caterpillars are a part of the process. Change lurks around every corner, and for growth to happen, you can't run from it. Instead, you must be prepared to tackle it head on with confidence.

I had found myself underwater, drowning from worrying about a situation that my oldest son, Eli, was facing. Kids are mean; that wasn't a surprise. But I didn't expect to have to prepare him for their next level of meanness at such a young age.

He was in first grade, and his biggest worry should have been memorizing his spelling words. Yet, I was trading in spelling practice for life skills, helping him build his toolkit to include coping mechanisms for dealing with bullies.

When his behavior began to change, I knew something just wasn't right. I pulled him aside one evening and after a little coaxing, he spilled the seeds, sharing everything about how he had been being treated by people he thought were friends. The only caveat to his open sharing was the pact I made to keep it confidential.

What's a momma to do when that's the prerequisite to sharing deep, dark secrets? For me it was harnessing the power of my breath.

If there is anything that can help you regain control when you feel like your life is spiraling out of it, it's taking control of one small thing at a time, and for me that always starts with my breath. I may not be able to control the situation or other's reactions or responses, but, as I assess and redefine what I have the power to impact in a stressful situation, I start by getting my body in the best shape it can be to focus.

The air around us is a gift offered to us.
Purposeful breaths are us actively accepting it.

A therapist later walked my son and I through a shared deep breath exercise. I watched as he closed his eyes and followed the therapist's directions. Deep breath in; deep breath out. As Eli and I took a few moments to savor the air around us, we learned the power of breath and its impact on shaking up our thoughts and grounding us. Extra oxygen also recalibrates our amygdala, the pesky part of us that doesn't think clearly when panic and worry are lingering.

That night, I took several deep breaths, consciously executing something that I do so often unconsciously. As I did this, I tried to focus less on the stressful situation and more on the tangible world around me. I heightened all my senses, turning on that which my body usually takes for granted. I made myself aware of where I was sitting, the smells of my surroundings, and the sounds that were naturally occurring that I may have previously overlooked.

Through each deep inhale, I'd let the air fill my lungs to capacity.
With each exhale, I'd push out my worries with purpose.
Only good mojo in; negative thoughts were forcefully evicted.

THESE SIMPLE, BASIC BREATHS WERE ANYTHING BUT SIMPLE FOR ME THAT DAY.

However, they became my sounding board in rationalizing the quantity of worry the situation at hand deserved.

By focusing my breath, I put life in perspective and found gratitude in the plants that cleansed the air I deeply inhaled. Without them fully knowing, they were helping with my situation.

For days, I honored our pact, knowing that the severity of the mean-ness wasn't putting his life in danger. I needed time to think, to strate-gize and to figure out my game plan. To uncover the best-case scenario, I had to take a moment to live in a worst-case scenario world. Most wouldn't expect this optimist to have such a heavy moment of realism, but thinking about things in the worst-case-kind-of-way tells my panic that the worst isn't quite as bad as it wants me to think it is.

I needed to think of the worst-case scenario, and that I did. In fact, I did worst-case scenario thinking on both sides of the situa-tion—what would happen if I never told anyone, and what would happen if I did and he found out.

After weighing the consequences, I opted to have a confidential conversation with his teacher, and together we created a new scenario, one that formed behind the scenes to set him up to steer clear of the meanness while I could prepare him from within to handle situations like these in the future.

It's been years since that day, and he's faced more meanness.
There have been others who pluck away his dreams.
There always will be people wanting to stunt your growth.

Petal pluckers, flower squashers and sunlight hoarders always exist. Instead of running from them, ensure your toolkit is prepared so you can grow anyway.

WHAT A PLANT NEEDS TO THRIVE ARE SIMILAR THINGS WE NEED AS WELL.

In fact, they help me focus on what matters when stress appears. I have several "go-to" outlets and depending upon my level of panic, I will use each independently or all of them collectively.

First in my line of defense is a bath. There is something about the extreme heat surrounding me that helps me feel comforted. As my skin turns red from the water's temperature, I find the tenseness within my muscles washing away. As my body relaxes, I take in several breaths and begin the worst-case scenario conversation in my head to work through the topic at hand (see how they all intertwine?!). Much like the bare-root strawberries, a bath tends to wake me up and reinvigorate me. What once felt overwhelming feels manageable afterward.

If a bath doesn't do the trick, I find a creative outlet, and I believe creativity comes in all shapes and sizes. I enjoy gathering fabric flowers or loose-woven burlap and making wreaths. Or I open my computer and let my thoughts flood on the computer page. With every word I type, the weight I carry feels lighter. The garden is always a welcomed solace for me, where I can pour out my frustrations in constructive manual labor, pulling weeds or digging in the dirt.

My oldest son's creativity is found on the basketball court, and my daughter's is most prevalent in her colored pencils. My youngest has game-changing moments when it's just him and Legos. Whatever it is, know what sparks the creative parts of your brain and use them in times when your creative energy needs to be called on. When you do, you may just find that you get creative at identifying solutions to your current concerns.

Sometimes, alone isn't the answer. You need to phone a friend, or in my case, call the teacher. Asking for help isn't a weakness, it's a strength.

STRESS WANTS YOU TO QUESTION WHAT YOU HAVE WITHIN YOUR SPAN OF CONTROL, HOPING YOU THINK YOU HAVE MORE THAN YOU REALLY DO.

It wants you to think you can pull out every thorny weed from your kid's interactions. It prays that you believe their struggles are direct correlations to your poor parenting. It gets a thrill when you cave, questioning who you are in the first place.

Stress doesn't want you to grow, it wants you to wither and wilt.

What is within your control is very limited. While it may sound depressing, knowing it is freeing. While you can control what you wear, what you say and who you interact with, you have no ability to directly control anyone else's thoughts. While you can control your work ethic, your education and your persistence, you can't control if you get the promotion, if you win the contest or if you have the innate skill set to achieve what you think you're supposed to. You can save every penny for the new house only for it to catch flames when you walk in. You can leave early to get to work on time only to get stuck in traffic after a wreck. You can plant the entire garden only for one frost to kill it all overnight.

I couldn't control that my son has already encountered mean kids in school, but I could control how I helped him navigate it. I couldn't control being impacted by corporate layoffs, but I could use my new-found freedom to take a risk and try a new direction I'd always dreamed of. I can't control what someone thinks of me, but I can control how I let that person's opinion of me impact my opinion of myself.

When you give up thinking you can control everything, you focus on only controlling one thing, *you*.

Then you realize that the situation that caused your life to unravel really wasn't the situation at all, but your reaction to it. Then you can give yourself permission to *grow through* what you *go through*.

Stress is inevitable.
Panic will show up whether or not its invited.
Anxiety is likely something you will experience at least once.

You can't run from it. You can't hide from it. But you can work through it and, in doing so, you can grow from it.

The Fort

All sports practices were unexpectedly canceled and so were our children's weekly swim lessons. Birthday parties were no longer on the calendars, offering opportunities for our kids to socialize with others. In fact, the social-distancing mandate of the pandemic called for new forms of socialization altogether. It was the first time in a long time we had a whole weekend as a family unit with no other commitments.

What were we to do with it? My husband and I had plans, and I soon found out, so did our kids.

Several weeks prior, my dad and I had spent a whole day at a plant nursery auction down the street from our kids' school. The company had been leasing the land that it had utilized for decades, and the owners opted to sell it for a retirement community to be developed. That meant all of the plants—from the littlest potted blueberry bush to the largest fruit tree—had to go. The owner of the nursery and landscaping company opted to coordinate an auction, so to the auction we went.

We had just moved into our new home, and we were more concerned with the house being finished than the landscaping being completed. We figured we'd get to it someday. But after a few months in and with spring on the horizon, we knew it was time to focus on our curb appeal. It was now or never. The auction was our opportunity, and after twelve hours of standing in the cold bidding on plants of all sizes, shapes and types, we left with a truck load of beauties.

THE PROBLEM WASN'T IF WE HAD ENOUGH PLANTS TO WORK WITH; INSTEAD, IT WAS WHEN WE WOULD FIND THE TIME TO WELCOME THEM INTO OUR HOME'S SOIL.

We had so much to do, so many commitments that took us away from our farm and didn't give us the chance to plant any beyond our fruit trees. We had found that the thirty minutes we had in the evenings before dusk to get a few bushes planted wasn't enough time. For weeks, the plants sat on the side of our driveway, yearning for soil and begging to grow.

With the early stages of confusion from the pandemic, everyone found themselves with time that they thought was once lost. We decided it was time to dedicate it to landscaping. The rain had held off, but the cold temperatures hadn't. We didn't care though; nothing was going to hold us back from our mission. Armed with scarves, gloves and hats to cover our extremities, Cory and I dug holes and planted to our hearts content.

While we were focused on the landscaping, our kids were into their own adventures on the farm.

At first, they found the mud piles. They didn't have to tell me that they found them because their mud-covered pants gave away their secrets. They walked like their feet were covered in cement—except it was mud that weighed them down—to tell us they were pivoting from the dirt mound to their next adventure.

THEY HAD FOUND A BROKEN-DOWN CABINET AWAITING ITS DESTINY THAT WE RELOCATED FROM OUR PREVIOUS HOME.

I remember that cabinet all too well, as it gave me the chills when we were packing it up nearly a year prior. It was originally filled with all things outdoor—from garden shoes to insect repellants, wood stains to screw drivers. It was the last item we packed for our move, and instead of putting everything in boxes (we were exhausted and fed up with packing by that time), we decided to move the unit as is, keeping everything within it for safekeeping until we were ready to unpack at our final destination, our new home.

The moment we moved the unit, I saw a visitor that had decided to make its final resting place our garage floor.

Under the white particle-board storage unit was a dead mouse. Who knew how long it had been there?

I jumped several feet in the air and refused to reenter the garage until someone got rid of it! Now, it was the cabinet that awaited its final resting place, in our next fire pit. The unit barely made it to our new home in one piece. Once we opened it to empty its contents, the walls began to cave in, so we knew it had done its job; it had completed its mission. Laying by our driveway were the walls of the unit, and when we went looking for wood for our next bonfire, we planned to burn its remains with it.

My kids had other plans though. While Cory and I landscaped, we heard their giggles and evidence of their imaginations running rampant. It was refreshing, especially since it meant that they were getting along (a feat we had been striving for!). After a while, Eli came begging for our help, and it was then that we took a moment to soak in what they had been working so hard on.

A fort. A castle. A clubhouse and a hideout. They had taken the broken boards awaiting their imminent doom and built something creative from it.

Together, they designed something special that gave the three of them a place to laugh and create. For hours they played with what Cory and I had set out for trash. While we had seen no more use for the storage unit's walls, our kids saw its ongoing potential.

WHY IS IT THAT THE OLDER YOU GROW, THE LESS IMAGINATIVE YOU BECOME?

When kids see a box, they see opportunity!
When I see a box, I see annoyance.

When they see a mud pile, they can't wait to climb it.
When I see a mud pile, I can't wait to demolish it.

When they see a ratty, broken-down storage unit, they see a fort.
When I see it, I see an eyesore.

Many times we think growing requires us to look up; but often it begs us to look down. My children look up to me to help them learn, but what if I took a moment to look up to them? What could they teach me instead?

That weekend was the beginning of immense change, for the pandemic had just scratched the surface. Poised for challenging times ahead, I was grateful for the reminder of the value of creativity and adventure, the joys found in the unknowns and the opportunities that awaited.

I didn't break down the newly created fort for a while. It remained a pile of trash to passers zooming by, likely questioning if we were a family of hoarders. But it didn't matter because to my kids, the cabinet had great value. And to me, it was a poignant reminder of the most unexpected of places that growth happens.

The Dam

The day he showed up with his gasoline-guzzling dually truck and an elongated trailer hitched to it, I knew he was up to absolutely no good. My dad loves farm equipment like writers love journals. While I have the pleasure of straddling farm life and author life, this day all I could do was shake my head, knowing he was about to embark on a project. And any project of his is one that becomes a larger-than-life journey for us too.

Perched proudly on the top of the trailer was a skid steer. The confidence this equipment had was breathtaking, and paired with my dad's eager smile from ear to ear, I knew that something exciting was on the horizon. Dad declared it was "pond day" and expected that my enthusiasm for the project would match his.

I was excited; however, my excitement was laced with the known truth that nothing Dad attempts to accomplish on the farm comes free from hurdles. In fact, I think farm life has a prerequisite for that.

If it isn't broken, it will break on the farm.
If it is easy elsewhere, it will take hours more here.
If it should only take an hour, it will take a month.

But here the pace is slower, and the air is thinner. Time slips through your fingers, and yet, a day can feel like a week. When I step out of my home and onto the land, challenges don't really feel like challenges. Instead, they appear like a welcomed opportunity. And extending the pond was one of them.

DAD HAD A VISION. IT WOULD ONE DAY BE A REALITY. BUT LITTLE DID HE KNOW, THIS PROJECT WOULD BECOME A MULTI-YEAR ENDEAVOR.

Our farm came complete with expansive land, a hidden creek gem and two spring-fed ponds that were underwhelming but full of potential. The front pond quickly became a meaningful piece of art that we view daily from our back windows. And the pond in the back of the property became the drinking well to wild critters of all kinds. While I wanted Dad to test the waters of dam building in the back first, where any mistakes would be easily hidden, he opted for the pond in the front to begin his learning.

Everyone does everything for the first time at some point. We walked for the first time, and that was pivotal so we could one day run. We mumbled some frivolous sounds, which became the basis of a spoken language. Dad hadn't extended a pond before, and he had to start somewhere.

If you don't live on a farm or aren't privy to knowledge about ponds, let me break down what this city girl has learned since moving to one. Not all ponds are God-made; many are man-made. I didn't realize this likely because I never contemplated it prior to moving to the middle of nowhere and realizing that our pond had suffered erosion over time and needed some TLC.

Some ponds are fully man-made, meaning those who got a lick of sense in how to tackle pond building dig a hole and let the rain fill it, crossing their fingers along the way, hoping the clay in the soil will keep the water at bay. Other ponds are lucky enough to stem from a spring found in the earth, constantly offering a replenished supply of water. Unbeknownst to me, this supply isn't flood level; it's a slow trickle that, too, needs nurturing. Without a bit of man-made help, the pond will never be what it could.

The latter was our situation. A measly pond just wasn't large enough for my fishing-loving pops. He had dreams—including one where he would sit on a gazebo resting in his reclining chair awaiting the bites of bluegill.

Never stand between my dad and his dreams because it won't work. The six-foot-two-inch burly man laughs when this five-foot-two-inch pipsqueak tries! The pond needed a dam, and Dad was going to make it happen.

He was methodical, especially for a guy who didn't have a clue what he was doing. He knew where to collect more soil to build a five-foot dam from corner to corner. He created a measuring stick out of a forgotten fence post and every day following would require myself and my husband to report on how many feet of water the pond was collecting.

DAY-BY-DAY, THE POND ROSE.

Each rainfall was welcomed in this household, for we knew it would make my dad squeal with excitement. God unzipped a massive cloud not too long after the dam was partially complete and we got to get a glimpse of what could be... if the dam held. But as quickly as the pond rose, it also retreated. Like the confidence one gets when they talk a big game, the pond cowardly shrank to its previous state when the rain wasn't consistent. A dance not for the weary, but one that to this day we still observe on a regular occurrence.

A glimpse of hope.
A reminder of challenge.

> Like the instinctive reflex of our inhales and exhales, the pond gets filled to the brim and then lets out a deep sigh as it begs for help.

The first time flash flooding approached our county, my dad called with anticipation, knowing we lived at the highest point of our area, and we were safe. But our pond, on the other hand, he wasn't so sure of. As much as we begged for rain, a flood could cause overflow, creating a dirt landslide, omitting the chance for settlement and increasing the chance of erosion. Alas, what we didn't want to happen did. Outside our picturesque back window we watched helpless as the pond gushed over the dam and knew no amount of will could stop it.

THE POND HAD TAKEN ALL IT COULD, AND IT, MUCH LIKE US, HAS A BREAKING POINT TOO.

We closed the blinds, believing that if we didn't see it maybe it wasn't happening, but you can't hide from overwhelm no matter how hard you try. It's still there, gushing and gushing and gushing.

The next morning, my husband and I visited the pond to see the damage. While one point of the dam was impacted by a bit of soil depletion, we were surprised to uncover that the pond and the abundance of water had created a pact, one that would last for years. Water has a way of uncovering the path of least resistance, so when given a moment to reflect, it relies on its memory for existence.

A slow but rising rain it can handle; a downpour is too much. (I hear you pond as I, too, commiserate.)

It identified a way around the dam, creating its own overflow plan, and it committed it to muscle memory. Now, when the air gets damp and the clouds burrow for a pow-wow, the pond and the water unite, preparing for a win-win option.

Saving the pond is a shared goal of all on this farm, pond and family included. But, as with most things in nature, the pond had another life lesson to offer.

A time of solace for me is on the riding lawn mower, where my worries are washed from me by the wind as I traverse uneven ground like I'm driving a race car. There is a peace found on a piece of equipment that leaves my body numb after using it to trim the unwieldy terrain of weeds and natural growing covering. With my Air Pods in and a business podcast turned high, I feel a level of free I don't feel elsewhere.

THE FIRST YEAR THE DAM JOINED OUR FAMILY, I FOUND MYSELF CONTEMPLATING A NEW CHALLENGE: HOW TO CUT THE GRASS CLOSE TO THE DAM WITHOUT PLUMMETING IN THE PROCESS.

It's a real fear for those of us who enjoy the rolling hills of the Blue-grass State. As I plotted a game plan for nearing the dam, I uncovered a hidden gem that was equally a newly chronic nuisance.

From the house, only one side of the dam is visible. But behind the dam—where the water would occasionally roar from overfill, overwhelm and an over-it mentality, were the most luscious grass blades ever found on our property. Thick and velvety. I would have rolled down that hill in it if I wasn't concerned I'd be joining a family of copperhead snakes along the way.

Abundant life lived on the other side of overwhelm, and it was something spectacular. The trek to get there was dangerous; the step of that dam was too tight to tackle on a riding lawn mower, that's for sure. But growth abounded and in droves.

As I shook my head, knowing that this posed a new challenge for cutting grass, I also smiled at the beautiful reminder of how life works. The pond and I are so, so similar, and yet, she continues to teach me more and more about life.

There is only so much we have the physical and mental capacity to hold at once. Sometimes, we can prepare for a capacity concern, asking for help and buckets to dig ourselves out of despair before falling into it. Other times, the flood warnings from our local TV station don't come quick enough for any form of preparation. All we can do is take a deep breath and pray that we have the muscle memory to find a path around it.

But sometimes nothing can be done. A sick child creates a domino effect in the family, leaving everyone out for the count during the week of a massive deadline and the in-laws are coming in to stay for the weekend. The pile gets bigger and bigger. The overwhelm feels like too much to carry. And even though you try, you can't always do it. Sometimes it just isn't possible. Welcome to life.

But even in those moments, something beautiful can and does happen. Hidden behind those moments is a lush path of life, so thick that you'll likely break a Weed eater trying to cut it down. Its beauty is breathtaking, but its purpose is bigger. Under the lush landscape is a web of roots doing all it can to help hold you together. It makes you stronger. It's reinforcing you without you knowing. Each root holds hands with the others, offering you a momentary reprieve from breaking all the way and only suffering from a slight overfilled situation.

THE DAM STILL LEAKS, AND IT DRIVES DAD BONKERS.

Regularly he approaches with a new idea to try to stabilize what is likely too much for one person to tackle. But much like his endless solutions that get us an inch closer to checking the pond project off the list, I'm reminded that maybe part of my dam is him and the others in my life. When I approach overwhelm, he shows up with a smile and massive piece of farm equipment to dig me out of it. Hand in hand, he helps me conquer what feels like too much to handle.

The dam isn't the solution; it's merely a lifeline. It doesn't stop everything; it just creates some breathing room.

It comes with challenges; but its purpose isn't to fix but rather teach you how to create muscle memory to work through the next flash flooding on the horizon. And believe me, it's already churning. This time, however, maybe you'll embrace the sound wisdom of the pond.

Create a pact with the water.
Together, uncover a solution.
And commit it to memory for next time.

See your floods as a tool to strengthen your dam, not destroy it. And rest comfortably knowing that life can, will and is growing because of it.

The Rest

Despite the swirling rumors, Cory and I decided worry wouldn't deter us; we were going no matter the outcome. We had already booked our anniversary trip to the Gaylord Opryland Resort in Nashville, Tennessee, and the impending layoffs looming at work wouldn't be cause to cancel it. Either way, the trip would be needed and worth every penny.

So much life had happened in the decade I worked for a nonprofit whose cause had become a vocation. I grew leadership skills while navigating piling responsibilities. Cory and I married early in my career with the organization, and our wedding video holds precious memories with peers I worked with at the time. Three maternity leaves welcomed each of our children during my tenure.

More than my blood, sweat and tears could be found in the hallways; the cause was deeply rooted in all I knew and in who I had grown to be.

BUT I WAS EXHAUSTED—MENTALLY, PHYSICALLY AND
EMOTIONALLY.

Over the course of ten-and-a-half years, my peers and I had been
through more change than my two hands could count, and the
onslaught of continued corporate downsizing was taking its toll on
everyone. I had reapplied for my own job and that of new positions to
ensure I had one each time.

Just when I got comfortable in the outcomes I was charged to deliver,
Change decided it was time for the reappearing part of a magician's
disappearing act. I held my breath for so long I didn't know I was only
taking shallow gulps, hoping I would make it through the next round
of corporate cuts.

This wasn't a way to live. I secretly questioned all parts of life, uncovering the true meaning of working to live, not living to work. I wasn't
living that adage in correct order, but I was aware my priorities
weren't in alignment, which was a step in the right direction.

> While change *can* be good, if it persistently nags, it can rob you of
> time with loved ones, passion for your calling and rest required
> for your body, mind and soul.

I was an equal financial contributor to our household, and while I was
terrified of losing my false sense of security, deep down, I was ready
for it all to end. If I made it through this round of layoffs, it would
leave me with more responsibility than one person's shoulders could
ever carry, and I was already unsteady with the current workload. If I
lost my job, our lifestyle would require major adaptations. I'd get a
new job, I told myself. We'd figure it out. One way or another, I determined, our trip to the gardener's paradise was going to offer rest and
rejuvenation.

We'd either celebrate making it through the layoff round, or we'd celebrate the newfound freedom the layoff provided. Either way, I needed a break, and there was no place better to take it. Our bags were packed; the trip was planned. And I received news my team was, in fact, being eliminated.

While grateful to have dodged previous layoffs, each prepared me for what was imminent. Many received similar fates that round (about 600 or so people) and were in tears; I, on the other hand, did an Irish jig. I needed a change, but I wouldn't jump all in without a push.

> Comfort had become a part of my identity, but nothing good comes from comfort. Change will always take down Comfortable in a wrestling match no matter who you are rooting for.

Change had won, and Comfort was on the verge of a mental breakdown. Even though I was ready for change, I needed to recalibrate, and Opryland was calling.

THE LUXURY HOTEL SPANS NINE ACRES, FEATURING 50,000 BITS OF TROPICAL FOLIAGE FROM AROUND THE WORLD.

The sight of the indoor gardens, complete with waterfalls and plants galore, is indescribable. The air is so pure, the experiences so memorable. During a previous river tour, our guide shared that the water we floated on was collected from bodies of water around the world, and foliage of all types lived in unison, thriving together.

In the warm months, blooms in the indoor gardens are abundant, offering eye candy at every glance. During the Christmas season, the grounds leave any Grinch with a full heart. That November, when we used the rotating doors to enter the land of living, staff were preparing for the season, stringing garland and twinkle light strands and adding ornaments to evergreen wreaths behind the check-in desks. My worries washed away with my first inhale inside.

Before settling in our room and securing dinner reservations, I couldn't contain my excitement any longer; I needed to take pictures. I find peace in the process of zooming into nature, so I pulled my Canon camera out of its case and hung it around my neck, like a true tourist. While Cory schlepped our luggage, my camera and I hunted for flowers. A sea of green enveloped me like a welcoming hug a grandma requires when coming to visit.

Hidden within the thick, manicured foliage were birds of paradise, a perennial native to South Africa. Resembling a tropical bird in flight, they were the only birds seen indoors, noticing bees, flies and other buzzing pests were missing as well. Peppered within other varieties were heart-shaped, lipstick-red flamingo flowers, also known as anthuriums. Occasionally I'd catch sight of a familiar favorite, the delicate cymbidium orchids, the centerpiece of our wedding flowers several years prior on that exact day.

With each shutter click, my breath adapted pace. The camera had its own heartbeat rhythm; it was retraining mine.

I had lived in one ongoing deadline, but a single phone call altered everything. My identity was lost, leaving me aimlessly seeking purpose alongside my footing. There was more to me than a job; but even though grateful for the layoff, I was unsure who I would be on the other side of it.

When introduced, most accompany a job title with their name as if it's a self-elected middle name. Sundays can be depressing, but only when you have Monday workdays to dread. If work wasn't a worry, what was I supposed to worry about in its place?

OUR WALK IN THE GARDENS FOLLOWED THE PATH
UNDERNEATH THE SECOND-STORY WATERFALL, ONE OF MY
FAVORITE SPOTS IN THE GARDENS.

Not only do you have the landscape surrounding, but you can peek
through the persistent stream from a unique angle. I stood under the
cascading flow, letting the gushing pulse drown my worries and
peered through the waterfall, both soaking up the scenery while
soaking in the water splashes. The new view offered new
perspectives.

Prior to that moment, the garden was so crisp I could count the veins
within the leaves. But through the waterfall, all was blurred. The occasional pops of colors from the tropical florals I took photos of were
now mixed with the hues of green, much like the acrylic blends my
children unintentionally create when forgetting to wash their brushes
between paintings. No longer could I identify the sought-after beauties; I had to merely trust that they remained nonetheless.

I came to the other side of the waterfall with a new outlook, on the
gardens and on life. The more I sought flowers, the less I found. Due
to the season, they were sleeping, hibernating until warmer weather
approached. When brighter days were ahead—and instinctively they
knew they were—they would reappear in droves. The blurred
painting of colors skewed green when looking underneath the waterfall, but in future months it would skew to shades of pinks and
purples, true colors reappearing.

This was their season of rest and mine as well.

Rest is a daily requirement. Even the sun embraces it.
Rest is a seasonal expectation. The trees let go of their past to prepare
for the future.

Rest conserves energy. Bears appreciate it each winter.
Rest restores energy. We can't fully function when sleep is lacking.

It's because of rest a plant can bloom when it's pollination time.
It's because of rest we heal from hurt and prepare for change.

That weekend, I didn't know my future. The months following, I listened, following my new path with ongoing trust. I questioned my steps at time, but never feared the outcome.

Growth, I learned, wasn't possible in comfort. Comfort binds our roots and hinders our growth.

Resting is not a luxury—even if you are resting in the memorable Opryland Resort. It's a necessity if you want to grow to your fullest potential.

PART FIVE

The Bloom

Beauty is in the eye of the beholder or found in the petals of a single flower bloom. Each petal is unique; all are immensely purposeful. While blooms captivate attention, their true intention is to inspire action. Life happens because of them.

Despite harsh conditions, flowers want to grow. Even in droughts—times when seeds fall on concrete—flowers find a way through the concrete cracks, seeking sun with unwavering hope to fulfill their calling.

Some of our blooms are eye-catching, turning heads and changing hearts. Others aren't as flashy, yet their purpose is vital. Our buds open when we encourage others to grow through what they're going through, seeing people where they are, who they are and loving them all the same.

A flower dreams of blooming.
I dream of helping others bloom instead.

The Work

Gardeners are as diverse as the seed packets they sow. My grandma, who had countless houseplants, was a flower nurturer. She was a gardener who loved planting beauties in landscapes. She knew the difference between perennials and annuals, planting accordingly to ensure each was cared for. She taught my mom when to prune rose bushes and which plants enticed the right insects to encourage pollination.

I learned a lot from my grandma, but let me be clear; that type of gardener I am not. Just peek at our front landscape and you'll realize I haven't a clue when to cut back anything. Without my mom's annual reminder, my landscape would be a hot mess.

Instead, I live on the other end of the gardening spectrum. I prefer the fruits of my labor to reap the nutritional benefit.

While I enjoy flowers, planting them usually makes little sense to me as after a few months, they go kaput. My planting of choice is tomato planting, strawberry pruning and cucumber vine weaving. I'm *that* type of gardener.

WHEN YOU ARE THE TYPE OF GARDENER I AM, PICKING WEEDS FROM YOUR LANDSCAPE FEELS LIKE A WASTE.

Save that energy to weed the vegetable garden, instead. I can't explain how weeds make it through tightly woven (and quite expensive) landscaping fabric growing at turbo speeds. Recycling newspapers stops weeds in my vegetable garden, but man-made nuisance barriers aren't quite as productive.

If I didn't know which type of gardener I was, I cleared up that question early one morning when the sun and my kids were still waking up. I had determined that was the ideal time to pick the necessary weeds out of our mulch. Frustration grew with each weed grab and root pull, realizing a task I had completed just days prior found its way back on my daily to-do list. Now, the unwanted pests were interwoven in boxwood bushes and monkey grass without ever getting permission to do so.

I typically didn't sweat the weeds except on days when company was coming over. And this day in particular, not just any company was coming over. Our first family home was on the market, and a potential buyer was hours away from meandering up the front walkway to consider if they saw themselves living in the home we had grown our family.

That day was important, and what do you do on important days? Pull the weeds.

The morning was quiet, but I had a persistent conversationalist nearby, myself. And any conversation between me, myself and I is unpredictable. That morning, I was debating the stupidity of weed pulling. I had a laundry list of countless other projects requiring my attention, and yet, there I was, pulling weeds I knew would resurface the day following.

What a wasteful task, and yet, there was something satisfying about each weed root I collected. It was as if the world's currency was in root exchange, and I couldn't collect enough. Each one I added to my collection felt more valuable than the one before.

AS WITH COIN CURRENCY, THERE IS ONLY MUCH JOY GREED CAN OFFER.

While the weed pulling was satisfying, something was missing. Even when I pulled out every sprout and our landscape looked as pure as the day it was planted, a piece of me was left unsatisfied, for I knew new weeds were awaiting below the dark depths of the landscaping fabric.

The job wasn't complete.
And it never would be.

I rested on the concrete steps leading to the front porch, gathering the courage to walk in the door, knowing good and well that when I did, the chore list for getting the rest of the house prepped for a showing would overwhelm me. For a brief moment, I soaked up the sun's rays, breathed in the morning's newness and received a lesson download from our Maker on the experience I had just endured.

In the stillness I saw a parallel between life and landscaping weeds.

With each I pulled, I realized how beautiful life would be if I took the same due diligence in weeding out the toxic relationships around me, the unnecessary worry that plagued me and the negative energy that creeped into my everyday life.

If I was as meticulous in identifying those who held me back as I was in finding the pesky weeds, I would feel a bit more satisfied than any clean landscaping could bring. If I put the same amount of care in what I chose to invest energy into as I did in ensuring my façade looked sellable enough, then I'd be golden.

Rest assured, just as weed pulling proves, if you don't maintain your relationships, your priorities or your personal habits, new weeds will resurface. Even when you put out landscaping fabric, toxicity can take root if you aren't prepped and ready.

Whether you're a gardener or not, know that you always hold the weeding tools. They may not look like a dandelion weeder or be as solid as a digging spade, but they can be just as effective and possibly even more so. For it's less about the tool and more about the intention. It's about your focus, and if you get to the root of what is holding you back and eliminate it from your life's landscape, you are destined to not be suffocated by your own weeds and be positioned to fully bloom.

The Move

～♈～

I knew it was a risk the day I brought her home. Some of my decisions I have immense confidence in; others I question the very moment I execute them. This decision was one I knew would likely not pan out the way I had hoped, but she was too beautiful not to take the risk anyway.

The African violet was potted in a simplistic planter, one that was industry standard and about as unexciting as flat paint in a builder-standard new home. The soil was begging for water, but her leaves looked strong, and the few measly flower petals she sported told me she was happy already; maybe she didn't require much to stay that way.

She offered me hope and showed promise. I was ready to give one of the hardest indoor house plants a good-faith try. Plus, how could I say no to her gorgeous, fuzzy leaves? (The simple answer is that I couldn't.)

If you have never met an African violet, let me sum up her horoscope. She is unexpectedly enticing but stubborn to the hilt. She is hard to please but when you do, you know it. While some houseplants are flexible, the African Violet laughs, mocking those for being too easy-going. She holds the winning baton for being strong willed. If she had eyes, she would absolutely out stare you in a staring contest just because she could.

SOMETIMES, I UNCOVER A PLANT'S ODDITIES AFTER I PURCHASE IT. BUT THIS ONE DIDN'T NEED A BACKGROUND CHECK.

I knew all about her from the beginning and decided to not give up on her, ever. Instead, I saw a lot of myself in her—a gal that knows what she wants and is willing to stand up for it no matter what—and I saw a lot of my grandma in her too.

In my grandma's modest apartment, I was unintentionally taught much about houseplants. Most of her plant collection sported different shades of green, so I would be elated during the holidays when her cactuses would bloom and when the African violets would decide they were up for showing their true colors. A humble handful of flowers would delight my grandma, and when Grandma smiled, I did too.

Grandma taught me everything about the African violet. Her leaves may be enticing, but never be tricked by her mockery. The oils from our fingertips could ruin her.

Let her be; that's all that she wants anyway.

When watering time, she also would never be seen with droplets on her leaves. They also harm the plant, so watering at the base of the plant, around her roots with a detailed eye to never touch her, is key.

She is one of those that prefers to keep to herself, never to be touched. If you even look at her wrong she wilts. And blooms? You're lucky if you ever see one, for she will only offer it when she's ready and most comfortable.

I HAD THE PERFECT PLACE PICKED OUT FOR MY AFRICAN VIOLET.

Her home was seated on top of a bourbon barrel, part of our Kentucky farmhouse decor. A succulent and rubber plant awaited their friend's arrival. I figured she would love her new home, especially since the pot actually read Home Sweet Home. But home is where the heart is, and for this plant, her heart had yet to be shown.

For three years I cared for her, sitting with her every Saturday during my watering rounds. I celebrated when new leaves sprouted and tried to get the rest of my family as interested in her growth as I was. Every bit of growth on her was a big deal to me. But a big deal to me was not a big deal to others in my house who just shook their heads at my addiction to cats and plants.

Yes, I am a crazy cat lady and plant lady. Not the best pairing—especially when one likes to eat the other—but you make do with what you have, I guess.

My grandma may have taught me about plants, but she had taught my mom first. So when I had a plant celebration, my mom tolerated my excitement. I counted down the days for Thanksgiving, the holiday where gratitude comes in the form of open bellies, not open wallets. No gifts required, just blessings, and we had our fair share of plenty. Annually, my parents join my family of five for a meal that leaves us waddling for days afterward, and this year was poised to do the same.

My African violet had been patiently growing in minute millimeters; however I found a few new leaves and was looking forward to showing my mom at dinner. The table was prepped, and the plant was positioned to be in her line of vision. I wanted her to see how I had kept this plant alive. She wasn't flourishing, but she wasn't dying. At least not yet.

While Mom and I celebrated while devouring the last piece of chocolate Derby pie, I nearly lost all of the calories I had just gained when I went to clear the table. Still perched on the bourbon barrel was the beautiful pot, but the plant was anything but.

It was as if she was attempting to do the downward dog position in yoga, because she was laying in all the wrong ways and only holding on by a mere root thread.

Her entirety was flopped over, face down in the soil, however no roots were exposed. Only one side of her stem was intact. She was holding strong, but I was fading fast. Three years it took to get her to this spot; just a few seconds for her to go down completely. No one fessed up to the situation, although I only asked the residents in our home who speak my language. My cats, on the other hand, had guilt all over their faces.

I FACED A FORK IN THE ROAD; A DECISION NEEDED TO BE MADE, AND I FEARED MAKING THE WRONG ONE.

Did I give the African violet the opportunity to keep holding on and see if she could get her footing again, or did I give up alongside her? With little to lose, I chose to flip her back and attempt to ignore what I knew was happening. Maybe if I didn't see it, I thought, it didn't happen.

Each day, I secretly slid over to her resting place to see if she was still alive. Her green remained strong, but her leaves began to curl. She wasn't getting the water she needed, but she wasn't giving up quite yet. And I figured I wouldn't either. I lifted her up, placing her broken pieces into a near-full cup of water, seeing if that would give her some life again. After a few days, I decided to repot her and pray.

I had every expectation that hope had been lost. I prepared to watch her leaves wilt and color slowly drain away. I didn't know what had happened, but I suspected the end was near. What did I have to lose? Nothing, I had determined, which is why I still tried anyway.

The days turned into weeks, and weeks turned into months. No growth was happening, but she wasn't giving up either. She was stagnant. She wasn't flourishing, but she held onto hope. One Saturday, I decided to rearrange our plants, which was a usual occurrence in our household. I had done a bit of online research to uncover that African violets preferred more sunlight than the original spot offered, so I decided to change things up.

A few of my plants had outgrown their previous spots, leaving an opening on our built-in shelves in the living room. I gently carried the African violet to the new opening of opportunity, and in doing so, I uttered to my husband the expectation for this to be her last week with us. Surely, I figured, the change would be too much for this stubborn cookie to withstand.

PEOPLE ENCOURAGE YOU TO TALK TO PLANTS.

They believe the positive words shared turns into positive energy that is received and reciprocated in return. Plants are living too, and words as well as sticks and stones can break them. But this African violet wasn't motivated by my words of discouragement; she was convicted by them. As with any temper tantrum toddler, she was determined to do the opposite of what I had predicted.

And she did.

Three days later, a few hours after the kids left with my husband for school and the house was enjoying the peace and quiet of the mid-morning, a little voice chirped when I walked by the shelves, encouraging a little look-see. Her outstretched leaves were reaching high, as if she was singing a worship song in silence. The forest green she had been wearing for three years straight just wasn't good enough for her new way of life now, as she glittered a vibrant green that only new plant life exudes.

She. Was. Happy. I could feel it as she shared it with me too. At that moment, we were both smiling.

Staring at her in awe, I had hit a new level of insanity since I had not only made a friend with my African violet, but I understood her deeply. I think it was because I, too, had just experienced the power of conditions and how they are the foundation for blooming.

There is a difference between surviving and thriving. Surviving is monotonous, like the ticking of a clock. Moment by moment, we exist. We move. We work. We breathe. We survive. Surviving merely requires just enough to get by; just enough to sustain where we are at this very moment.

But thriving is next-level goodness. It's not just moving; it's moving with purpose and pizazz. It's not just working but filling one's day fulfilling one's purpose. It's not just breathing but being cognizant of our breath and ensuring what we breathe, what we think, what we say and what we do is aligned with where we need to go.

To thrive, we need to up level the conditions we need to survive. For my African violet, she had a home. She had enough soil and got watered regularly. She even held on by a thread when life became unwieldy. But the move giving her even just a bit more light reinvigorated her to grow, even though she regularly considered giving up altogether.

What do you need to do to up level your conditions? Is it who you surround yourself with? Or what you watch or listen to? Is it your job or the current dating scene?

The path toward blooming, as my African violet will now tell me, isn't the big changes but the small ones. It isn't the new pots but the familiar ones. It isn't greener grass; it's merely a move to the other side of the room where you can get a new perspective, a bit more sunlight and a reminder that even though you get to choose where you bloom, you can grow from where you are planted too.

The Whole

~~~

The day held promise, but that promise was quickly robbed the moment I veered my vehicle onto the interstate. I was hearing words of constructive feedback on the other side of the phone when I was jolted forward, grateful for the securely fastened seatbelt. I saw the cars ahead of me slow quickly, brake lights glowing from all directions. I was confident in my brakes as they brought my car to a screeching halt too.

But before I could let go of the breath I unexpectedly was holding, I heard crunching metal when the car behind me hadn't been as successful as I in adhering to the unforeseen traffic jam. In fact, it had actually made matters much worse.

There I sat on the busiest interstate my city had in a multi-car pileup. No one could get out of their vehicles for fear of the zooming cars rubbernecking at our misfortune and saying prayers of blessings under their breaths that they weren't the ones stuck in the place we were.

Awaiting for the police to arrive to sort out the situation, I cried tears of stress and worry. I knew I should have been grateful I was alive as were those in the same predicament, but instead, I was debating something much more than who was going to pay for my car's damages.

THE CONSTRUCTIVE FEEDBACK I RECEIVED ABOUT A BOOK I FELT CALLED TO WRITE WAS PROVING HARDER TO DIGEST.

I had expected to receive positive accolades from early readers, but instead a select few had areas of opportunity they wanted me to explore. I was tired because every ounce of me was scribbled across those pages. I wanted to fold, wave my white flag and bow out. I questioned why I wrote, why I worked to share the good, why I did any of it. And the day I got my car back from the repairs it suffered from the wreck, I found my other car face-to-face with a neighbor's mailbox after I borrowed their driveway to turn around.

Writing had been my soul's glue, but at that moment it wasn't the super glue type I needed. It appeared to be the cheap dollar store version that never holds anything together no matter how much you beg it to.

I was responsible for tying my frayed threads together in hopes I wouldn't unravel completely. And I figured what better place to go and look for more thread than church; so to church I went.

Since kindergarten, Fridays during the Lenten season have been earmarked for father/daughter time. While my friends would run around our church's fish fry, telling secrets and gossiping about their crushes, my dad and I would be deep in prayer, inhaling incense instead of fried fish goodness. Most see Lent as an opportunity to give up something they should have given up years ago; my dad and I took something on instead. If Jesus had to carry his cross, we would carry it alongside him each Friday by participating in our church's Stations of the Cross.

The fourteen stations are symbolic of the journey Jesus took the day of his crucifixion. His steps were heavy, for he knew what was in store. However, even among the tears of his dedicated followers, he also knew what was next. That Easter day, life as he knew it and we knew it would be forever changed. Over the decades my dad and I participated in Stations together, my understanding and appreciation for them deepened.

Maybe it was because of my spiritual maturity; maybe it was because I could invite my family to come and experience it too.

At that time, before the service began, my family would meet up to scarf our fill of cheese pizza, macaroni and cheese, fried pickles and fish. After our bellies were full, we would split up. The kids were still little, so Cory would take the boys to the cry room to get out their pent-up energy from the day, and Lyndi and I joined my dad for thirty minutes of reflection as we celebrated every station of Jesus's journey to the cross.

My daughter flipped through the hymnal that night while the rest of us did the ritualistic genuflect-stand-kneel Catholic routine. Occasionally she whispered not so softly while asking about items she noticed around the church. She was enamored by the stained-glass windows, trying to depict the items in each. She was excited to find a dove and tried to draw my attention to it. I redirected her to see the statue of Jesus instead, and her eyes lit up. After all fourteen stations were complete, we gently dabbed our fingers in holy water and wrapped up our evening with the sign of the cross. She wrapped three fingers of hers around my pointer so we could walk together safely to our van and head home.

Before her lips parted, I could tell she had a question. She never had to ask, since I already knew the answer. "Yes, sweet Lyndi," I said. "You can pick a flower."

OUR CHURCH HAD A TON OF THEM THAT SPRING DAY— WEEDS THAT IS.

While typically a dandelion would suffice for Lyndi, she had become especially fond of our church's weeds because they had an abundance of purple ones. Each Sunday she would look through the grass for a perfect one to pluck from its residence to take home and savor, and this night was like any other. What was most comical, however, about her flower picking skills at that age was that once she plucked her perfect one, her plucking wasn't complete. She had to pluck every beautiful purple petal off too until she was just left with the green stem only. It was only then that she was most happy holding her measly flower stem. Pitiful to the naked eye, glorious to hers.

She completed her flower demolition before we got in the car, and so proud of herself, she held her green stem with a smile as she sweetly gazed out the window on our short drive home. The vehicle was quite quiet, and I welcomed it since I was still reflecting from the mistakes of my day. Then she broke the silence with her sweet, little child voice.

God offers messages just when you need to hear them from a person who is the best to deliver it. He knew, at that very moment, the only way to get to me was through a direct message from the littlest voice available. I hadn't been in the mood to hear what he subtly placed around me, so a thundering cloud it was.

My head was spinning trying to figure out the cost of the mailbox I just smashed and the sideview window I would have to fix. In the true multitasker fashion that I am, I was also stressing about work and other challenges that had been laid before me. I was dwelling on everything broken in my life; yet at that moment I couldn't see the one thing in front of me that wasn't.

From the backseat, Lyndi held out her flower and said, "Momma, this flower is breakable."

"Yes, sweetheart, it is," knowing all the plucking she had just done.

"Momma, I love my flower."

"I know you do." She didn't tell a lie. And she loved hard.

"Momma, we're breakable too. You and me. We are breakable."

I was speechless.

"We're breakable, Momma, but we aren't broken. Nope."

As quick as she started, she stopped. The car fell silent once again after I had agreed with her wisdom by exchanging a smile and a few nods, and then she returned to gazing out the window, as if she didn't recall the depth of the message she just delivered.

LENT IS A SEASON OF SADNESS. JESUS SUFFERED TRAGICALLY, EXPERIENCING HUMAN PAIN ALONG THE WAY.

He was tortured and beaten. He was pushed to the ground, and just when he probably didn't feel like he had an ounce of energy left, he knew no one here could break him. They tried, breaking his legs and puncturing his ribs. They did everything they could to break his body, but his spirit would never shatter. No pain on earth, no challenge he faced, no struggle he endured... he would persevere.

He proved that our bodies are breakable, but through God we will always be whole.

My multi-car pile-up could have resulted in a hospital visit. Instead, my car saved me from everything but a lingering headache and later saved my husband from hydroplaning off a country road into an embankment he shouldn't have walked away from. The mailbox could have taken more of a beating, and our van too, but it didn't. Less than twenty dollars and my pride aside, I was able to fix that broken mailbox for our neighbor. I'm lucky the mailbox was all that took that beating; I could have hit someone flying down our street unintentionally. But none of that happened. My breakable body was left whole. For a reason I'm sure God will one day explain.

Until that day when I meet our Maker, all I have are messages he sends in the body of a sweet little girl who reminded me what matters most.

The world can pluck away what you deem beautiful. It can rob you of your petals and make you feel like you are worth nothing, deserve nothing, are nothing. But it is then that God loves you the most.

He sees you for who you are at the core. He knows that your shell is breakable—it can shatter—but when you have him in your heart, nothing, and I mean nothing, will break you. With him you are whole.

The next week, I headed back to church for the last of the six weeks of Stations tradition that year. I scarfed down more fried food than my body would care for and my kids all devoured a shared piece of chocolate cake they begged for each week. Lyndi stood next to me during the service, and afterwards, she begged to pick another flower as usual. But that time I smiled as she removed what everyone else sees as the beauty of it, so that she could find the true beauty behind it all.

I watched her cherish that green stem, remembering that that's exactly how God cherishes us.

You are never broken.
Breakable, yes. Our bodies are that.
But broken, never.

Remember that with God you are always whole.

The Overlooked

Y ou've heard the phrase: a family that prays together stays together. But what about if a family adds other things to that list? What about a family that eats together or watches movies together? Hopefully that will also deepen their bond. And how about a family that hikes together too?

I figured if praying and staying are bound together tightly, then maybe hiking and liking do as well. And if both happen at once—praying and hiking—maybe it would be the cherry on the top of the family banana split? Or maybe I was just looking for a reason to trudge my favorite four on a charge I had been seeking. Maybe they were to be my hiking accountability partners?

Not only does my body feel better after a walk in the woods, but my soul does too.

So, I asked my family to join me on a weekly hike one summer because I needed it, and I was hoping a healthy side effect would be a deeper bond with all of us too.

We ventured to the beautifully manicured little park in the downtown of our tiny city right next to the itty-bitty post office. You could over-look it in a blink as you zoomed by in the car if you weren't aware of its presence. I know I had time and time again before. Louisville is proud of its surround sound parks that outline the city's outer limits, so we leashed up our dog and traveled to several of those parks too, each more beautiful than the next. But my favorite destination was a hidden gem on the other side of the Ohio River.

ROSE ISLAND WAS ONCE A BOOMING ATTRACTION.

In the 1920s, it came complete with an amusement park, a hotel, a swimming pool and caged animals offering visitors a unique treat away from the city. With Charlestown, Indiana, as its home base, families would hop on a steamboat after church and enjoy a picnic and more together. However, the 1937 flood submerged the park, leaving its owners in a financial pickle with no other choice than to close its doors.

For a hundred years, it's remained vacant. A blast from the past, remnants of the star attractions remained, I had been told, and the state had created a park surrounding it where people could hike and enjoy.

Living outside of Louisville, where Waverly Hills Sanatorium—one of the world's top ten most haunted places—exists, I get excited when I hear of an abandoned place that is open to exploration. You never know what you will uncover.

One Sunday, we packed our bags with snacks and plenty of water and made the trek to Rose Island, the abandoned amusement park. We had little expectations, as we hadn't researched prior to pulling into the park's parking lot, which I suspect was a good thing since the hike to Rose Island came with plenty of warnings. Due to the steep incline and distance required to reach the amusement park and the complete abandonment of it, people were encouraged to not make the hike, for if they were unable to make it back up the hill to the lot afterward, there was no one available to be of assistance.

Just like you overlook a bear warning sign on a trip in the mountains, hopeful that you aren't one of the few who actually encounter one, Cory and I did the same with the hiking warning, figuring we could take breaks if needed.

Surely we had enough stamina to make the short hike. Our shoes were tightly laced, and our spirits were high as we began with no intention of turning back, despite the pleas from our littles. It builds character, I thought, as we began the steep descent to the hidden gem of an experience.

THERE IS SOMETHING BIZARRE ABOUT BEING IN THE MIDDLE OF THE FOREST, AWAY FROM THE CONSTANT STIMULI THAT ELECTRONICS OFFER NOWADAYS.

You begin to see with new eyes, and your ears hear things that normally it tunes out. I could hear the singing of a cardinal, the single bird that has become my best friend since my grandma's passing. I could hear the wind, the only reminder of its presence since the only other visible sign is the movement of leaves or hair in your eyes when you would prefer it to stay in place.

Each step down the slope was methodical, and it was as if my shoes were holding a simultaneous conversation with the pavement in gratitude for its support in keeping us stable during the hike.

Parallel to the rhythm of nature happening within arm's reach, our conversations, too, had begun to deepen. My oldest began to delve into deep conversations about life while my daughter sang as if she were joining in the cardinal's melody. It was a new level of peace; one that I had been in desperate need of.

Occasionally, my daughter and youngest son would yelp in excitement for a new flower or plant we hadn't seen before.

"Momma, we have to get a photo of this one!" became a sentence on repeat as I would snatch photos of the wildflowers beaming with pride of their simplistic beauty.

The hike to the abandoned amusement park was, indeed, worth every single step. After crossing a modern bridge, the moment we stepped foot on a piece of historic land it felt like we were transported back to a time when things we take for granted were cherished novelties.

We walked in the park's swimming pool, which now is filled to the brim with soil and covered in grass. In the distance I could almost hear the splashing of the water like I do when my kids are drawn to a pool.

We walked by some forgotten metal half buried into the soil, but after reading the plaque stationed nearby, we learned that it was all that was left of the cage that Teddy Roosevelt, the park's black bear, called home. Our youngest jumped in for a photo opp.

We saw where the hotel once stood before the waters consumed it, and from there you could see the dock where boats would drift in, filled to the brim with the excitement of visitors for a day getaway. We found a stump by the previous dock that offered a momentary reprieve as we imagined what life was like back then.

The consistent pace of the water's motion reminded me that what was and what is will always be. Maybe what was wasn't so different from what it is today.

We walked past remnants of a place once filled with laughter and memories to what could only be explained as a hidden ghost town in an old Western movie. Except horses would have rejected the request to make the steep trek, abiding to the strong warning signs of the hike down. Very little was left of the previous park, but the land held the memories close, refusing to give up any, much like a dog is insistent to keep his bone close.

The soil knows of the steps once taken, and the trees remember the secrets children shared. What may appear as forgotten land is anything but.

Once every landmark sign was read, every concrete block was touched and every hiking trail was explored, we gave our feet a pep talk for the hike back to the van. Going down was a piece of cake. Going back wouldn't be quite as easy and there was no grandma's house to end up at even after we went through the woods and over the river.

To keep our minds preoccupied with positive thoughts and not drowning in negative frustrations from the pain of uphill hiking, I continued the challenge for our family to find the coolest flowers possible to capture photos of. When you take something seemingly insurmountable and make it small, attainable even, you can smile through the sweat and celebrate through the muscle aches.

We had relished God's beauty on the path toward the amusement park, but our focus was even more granular on the way back, and because of it, we saw even more. The forest weeds—ahem, wildflowers—were abundant. Shades of lavender and pearl white begged for our eyes to see them and all their beauty. Abundant butterflies danced from petal to petal as if they had taken swing lessons and were showing off their new skills to their friends. It was a sight I'll always cherish.

MY FAVORITE FLOWER, HOWEVER, WAS A SEEMINGLY SIMPLE WHITE ONE THAT LOOKED LIKE A DANDELION'S COUSIN.

With a strong stem, it held its head high and confidently sprouted little bunches of white petals not much bigger than the tip of a gel pen. At first glance, I overlooked it as I'm sure most passersby had done. It was the forgotten of the wildflower friends, the outcast of the crew. But I was drawn to it and got close to take a photo of its brilliance, naming it the Snowflake flower. And yet, the closer I got, the more I saw.

What first appeared as a single white flower was actually a bouquet of dozens living off of a single stem. Upon closer inspection even the petals had a level of intricacy that was miraculous.

I stood in awe, almost as if I had seen a ghost but instead, I was taking in the level of detail God had constructed into something so few ever would actually see. I called my kids over to the flower, and together we sat there speechless at its humble beauty.

"If God takes such care to make these tiny flowers so intricately beautiful, never question how purposeful each and every part of you are."

It was the only bit of wisdom I could find the words to say before we continued our walk up the steep incline. Even though the conversation flowed with every sweaty step up to our van, I couldn't shake that single flower.

I had dismissed it as a weed at first… or a wildflower that I would just ignore. In fact, I'm confident I had seen relatives of it in other parks, on other hikes, deep in other forests. But it was the intentional moment we had that opened my eyes to it, enticing me to lean in and see the perfection of each mini flower within the collective. It was gorgeous, purposeful and magical all in one.

Hours later, after taking a steaming hot bath to calm my aching muscles and clean off the sweat stench, I opened my phone to savor the memories from our afternoon hike. I reminisced about the rich history we learned as a family, and while scrolling through the photos, I felt the flower calling my name. It had more to tell me, and since we spoke different languages, I needed to zoom in to hear it more clearly. As I did, I noticed a whole new world working in parallel to mine.

On this single flower were at least twenty bugs that called it home.

I was equally amazed and full of gratitude. I was in awe of the little bugs living on what I learned was called Queen Lace. And at the same time, I was thankful we opted to not pick it and invite those bugs home with us. Instead, what I did bring home was a reminder that nothing God makes isn't perfect, purposeful and interconnected.

That is true for the flowers.
And it's true for you and me as well.

To the naked eye, we may feel overlooked and ignored, but upon examination, we are each meaningful, and God only makes amazing stuff! His level of artistry isn't one Picasso could out paint. His attention to detail is greater than any perfectionist's. His creative eye is more innovative than anything we could ever attempt to create, for he forged the Grand Canyon, and he designs artwork deep underwater in the Great Barrier Reef. There isn't a place where his fingerprint isn't visible.

Next time you see a weed, don't overlook it, for it may be God's gentle reminder to you that you matter more than you know.

The Comeback

~∽~

My grandma was a lover of many things. Strawberry Pop-Tarts and ramen noodles were her go-to when we grandchildren would spend the night at her house. Her pockets were always filled with tissues and peppermints, which came in handy when flying in an airplane with her and needing a spearmint to calm a queasy tummy. She had more matching jogging suits than any one person could own, and her bathroom cabinet was always stocked with toothpaste, shower products and Bath and Body Works lotions.

She could probably have created her own Bath and Body Works store in her home with how much she acquired. But we loved it, and we loved her.

She smelled as sweet as she was, and her skin was as soft as the fresh cotton scent she sported.

I am sure I first smelled the scent of lilacs from her lotions. The soft scent became synonymous with spring when I walked in her home, and I was excited when we snatched three lilac bushes and two lilac trees at the nursery auction for our landscaping. The shrubbery was hibernating when we won them at the auction, so we hadn't a clue what we had really purchased until the following year when they bloomed.

The three bushes were planted outside of our bedroom window, with the goal of them merging one day to create a lilac hedge. The two trees bookended a row of boxwoods and azaleas along the side of our garage. Everything was tiny when we planted them, but each quickly took root, and that year's spring rain was a blessing in disguise.

The way our house is situated, it's uncommon to enter or exit the front door. In fact, the only time I enjoy the sights of the beef cattle grazing across the street is when I water the flowers gathered on our front porch pots. With a full watering can in hand, I opened the door to the sweetest aroma; the lilac bushes had bloomed, and boy did they not disappoint. With purple blossoms throughout, the bees were just as elated as I was to savor in their beauty.

If the bushes had bloomed, surely the trees had too, and as expected, the scrawny trunks proudly sported the most gorgeous lilac petals as well.

Purple versions of Dr. Suess's Truffula tree puffs, I became as impassioned as the Lorax was to save them anytime a spring tornado warning was cued. It wasn't the wind, however, that ever hurt the trees; instead, it was our dog.

SOME ANIMALS YOU ADOPT; OTHERS ADOPT YOU.

Tom showed up in our barn, terrified and starving. The gray-and-white fluff ball is the only cat I've met that can meow, hiss and purr at the same time. Never able to acclimate with our indoor cats, she determined our garage was her forever home whether we liked it or not. Good thing we love it because we love her and all her quirks.

Zoey is a fluff ball too, but more of the cotton ball edition. A Great Pyrenees and Retriever mix, she is the biggest teddy bear known to mankind. When we moved to the farm, Cory matter-of-factly stated that every farm needs a farm dog. While I love all animals, I know dogs require more work than cats, and I had become accustomed to the relaxing cat parent life. Cory, however, never felt settled until the day he called me with the news.

A family member of a patient of his had a stray dog that had a litter of puppies a year prior. The momma and one puppy remained, and while the family had plans on keeping the momma, the puppy still needed a forever home. I figured there was a reason the lone ranger hadn't been picked. After meeting her, though, I knew it was because she was always meant to be ours. Her chocolate eyes tell stories that only she and I experience together when she rests her chin on my blanket at nights silently asking for a piece of popcorn. A lover of the outdoors and all people, she's the perfect addition to our zoo.

But just because you love someone doesn't mean they don't upset you. And Zoey and I didn't speak for days after she broke one of my trees in half.

I DON'T KNOW THE HOW OR EVEN THE WHY. I JUST KNOW THE OUTCOME.

The David-sized tree was broken in half by the Goliath-sized dog. Half of the trunk remained, and broken with the tree was also my patience. My perfectionist tendency felt off kilter, unsure that we could find another tree to oppose the last man standing that matched it. I opted to ignore it for the rest of the year, and instead, just gave

Zoey evil glances as if that could press the rewind button and fix the problem.

I figured we'd need to find a new tree the following year, one that didn't try to be like the others since matching wasn't possible. With a deep sigh, I let go of the would-ofs and could-ofs and just moved on like life would anyway. Secretly, however, I noticed it every single day, and cried a little pity party alone. Much like when the kids break something, Zoey didn't do it on purpose. Too bad, however, she didn't have a bank account to pay for the damages.

The next spring, it was time to put another layer of mulch on our landscaping. We purchased some flowers to complement the greenery and got to work, with the aroma of lilacs wafting in the wind, offering us moments of surprise and delight while we dug in the dirt and spread mulch like champs. We made it to the first tree and noticed a bird's nest meticulously built within it. A few eggs had been laid, proving that more called our place home than just us.

With every mulch bag we broke open, we got closer and closer to the eyesore, the stick erected from the soil at the end of landscaping. Prepared to just dig it up, I held a shovel in my hands when I noticed new growth. At the base of the tree, nearly naked to the eye, was a green leaf. No branches existed. No limbs were left. But the tree wasn't done. It was ready for a comeback. And that year it did.

Sprouting new limbs at the base, that year the tree began to grow and spritzed itself with the same lilac perfume as its partner in crime, although they were no longer shaped like identical twins.

Cut from the same cloth, each now beat to different but still beautiful drums. What was about to be discarded wasn't ready to stop blooming; it had and still has so much life to live and give.

Plants are resilient. Their growth is not always in the way we'd like, but they are living proof that there are many paths to similar destinations and no one path is the right one to take. Even when others give up on them, they don't give up on themselves. They know their worth and they work hard to keep it.

Embody the lilac tree's resilience; never give up even when broken. Embrace growth's timing; rest in the season, knowing another is near. Enjoy the beauty of a comeback; there is always room to bloom.

PART SIX

The Pollen

Is life about the seed, waiting to break free and break through?
Is it about growth, seeing challenges as fertilizer?
Is it about the bloom, where we stand loud and proud in our colors?

The seed is where we start, but the pollen is where others do.

We are an interconnected part of nature, meant to give as much and if not more than what we take. Our growth isn't meant for only us; it's a part of the living community that we are a part of. It's the people before who have shaped the now. It's those of us today who pollinate tomorrow.

A plant's true purpose is to give so that everything it touches has the chance to grow as well. Don't strive to merely bloom; seek to always pollinate.

The Treasures

Some people are blessed with knowing their pre-destined path in life, almost as if it were served to them on a silver platter with a five-course meal. As if their purpose was delivered by their local mail carrier in a beautifully packaged box, and all they have to do is pull the string for the ribbon to release its contents.

Maybe they were born with it written on their birth certificate right next to their length and weight—six pounds, fifteen ounces, twenty-one inches long—Purpose: Changing the world.

Wouldn't that be lovely? Knowing exactly what you are supposed to do, where you are supposed to go and how you are supposed to make an impact from the moment you exit your mother's warm and secure nook and are welcomed into our chaotic world? Wouldn't it be a beautiful baby shower gift if your parents' friends gifted them with your life's roadmap to happiness instead of a box of diapers destined to be soiled?

While some people realize their calling at an early age, for most of us it is a quest we embark upon the moment we let out our first cry. Instead of that cry being associated with the temperature change, it's our cry for help, a cry to not just have someone else physically come to our aid, but our cry to God to help lead us purposefully.

FOR MORE THAN A DECADE POST-COLLEGE, I MEANDERED ON THE PATH I THOUGHT I WAS SUPPOSED TO TAKE.

Working with nonprofit organizations meant I was mission-focused, but I found my passion being zapped more and more each day. The bureaucracy of any organization will take its toll on you if you let it, and even though I was determined not to—for the purpose of making a difference in a cause that had hit too terribly close to home—it wiggled its way in and took root in my life.

I was no longer fulfilled.
I no longer felt valuable or valued.
I wanted to give up.

I went through the motions, which consisted of the daily monotony of work and parenting, peppered with an occasional outing to fuel a hobby I had picked up. In the midst of traversing the path I thought I was supposed to be walking, God plopped something else in my lap— the charge to write a book. I didn't know why he felt so strongly that he needed me to write my story, but every time I tried to focus more on my career and less on his calling, I felt him at my back, poking me with his finger until I caved.

Fine. I'll do it. And I did, begrudgingly.

He wanted me to write, so I would write. I didn't know what about, but slowly he told me. He told me through my career challenges and parenting failures. He told me through the voices of others who would share with me their takes on the world. He told me through the squeaks of my young kiddos. And when he wanted me to publish this book, he didn't let me walk away when I wasn't sure how to afford it. That's when I finally received his roadmap, and boy was it completely different from what I would have ever imagined.

A WREATH MAKER.

While working a full-time job that already left my cup overflowing, he called me to write messages he placed on my heart and build a wreath business alongside. If you know me now, this wouldn't surprise you, because you know the end to the story. It isn't quite so outlandish to think I would have done what I did unless you knew the me before. I had only made one wreath prior to this, and it was no Martha Stewart beauty. But that Christmas after I prayed about how I would find the finances to write and publish a book, he placed in my heart the desire to make a burlap wreath for my brother-in-law and his family as a welcoming feature for their new home.

I hadn't made one before, but where there's YouTube, there's a way! After cranking out my first, I was impressed with my handiwork, having learned a skill I didn't know I had. I was so excited, I posted it on social media, because, you know, there's nothing like getting a little crowd validation. I never expected that one post could have the power to change a life, but it did mine.

If life had a fast-forward button, I would have used it, wanting to know where a hobby I didn't know I had would propel me. But at the time, all I had was faith and a healthy dose of it.

In mere months, I was able to raise the money needed for my book to become something real.

But I wasn't given a fast-forward button in my box of purpose from God. I didn't know the wonders he had in store or the mountains I had to hike to get to them. The only reality I got on top of custom wreath orders was a new friendship with the local craft stores, and this friendship wasn't a surface level kind of one. My relationship dug deep as each custom wreath order pushed me into new creative territory.

THE CRAFT STORE BECAME MY HOME-AWAY-FROM-HOME.

If I wasn't tucked in my house's nooks, I was winding a cart through every craft aisle collecting materials like I needed to hoard them like people did toilet paper at the dawn of the pandemic. I found freedom in this crafter's dream haven; my kids, on the other hand, boycotted attending.

It was as if passing through the sliding doors and breathing the craft store's circulated air they would contract the plague, or worse, they would have to endure monotony as their momma pondered flower color combos. They didn't endorse this career shift and begged to not join me on my material collection adventures. Well, two out of the three of them did at least. My daughter, on the other hand, had her life's purpose built into her psyche from day one, and little did I know our crafting experiences were meant to thrust her to put her mission into action.

A grumpy trio of littles were greeted by a chipper store employee one afternoon during an unwanted-but-required craft outing. She saw my patience fading and opted to throw this momma a bone.

As they bickered about who got to sit in the cart and who had to walk alongside holding it, she diverted their attention to something she had picked up off the floor. It was Christmas season, so she had a part of a red, glittery berry stem in her pocket she had rescued from the floor expecting to toss it in the garbage. That is until she decided to put my kids on a quest, and her plan worked.

She gave the glittery trash to my daughter and challenged the kids to look for more hidden treasures around the store. A new adventure awoke, and it was as if creative trash was as valuable as a pirate's hidden treasure. Each kid, but my daughter especially, would now light up when I brought up the dreaded craft-store outing—not because of their excitement for neon-colored felt, fabric flowers or loosely-woven burlap, but for their love of hidden gems.

THE FALLEN BEAUTIES THAT EVERYONE ELSE TOSSED BECAME VALUABLE CURRENCY IN OUR HOUSEHOLD.

My daughter collected all types, but her most favorite were broken fabric pieces, colored to give the perception of being a life-like flower petal. As people would pick up artificial flowers to observe, deciding if they would purchase, it was inevitable that there would be a fallen soldier; that one of the petals would lose its place and fall onto the floor, never to see its original stem and petal pairing again. Lucky for it, if it was a day that we stopped by, Lyndi would save it from the depths of despair and offer it a new job, a new purpose.

For years, she had a ridiculous amount of fabric flower "waste" in her room. All colors, all varieties, all originally seen as trash, but to her, valuable treasure. Initially, I laughed off her newest hoarding addiction until I saw her use it to help change the lives of those around her.

My daughter didn't come with her purpose on her birth certificate; instead she had it painted on her face in the form of a constant smile.

Her purpose—to make others smile—was so baked into her DNA that she suffered speech delays from what her therapist acknowledged as weak mouth and tongue muscles. All of her smiling negatively impacted the appropriate muscles in her face, which helped her form words. But she didn't let that stop her from her life's mission, and if her speech was cumbersome, she would find another way—through her flowers.

It started when I would come home after having a sour day. She would go missing for a few moments, returning with a broken flower petal, gifting it to me to cheer me up. It then extended to bringing surprise gifts to her siblings and grandparents, special touches just when each needed them. She would drop them into gift bags before birthday parties without my knowing and strategically place them around the house, hidden from the naked eye, but purposeful, for when you found one, you knew her intentions.

Until she outgrew her love for this endeavor, I kept her little flower petals around the house, just where she placed them, as they offered daily teaching on the purpose that each of us have and the charge we are given to share it with others.

During that time, I was impacted by a corporate layoff. I found the flowers a reminder that just because I was leaving a career I had found success in, one I thought was the path I was supposed to be on, didn't mean I had to feel lost. Being laid off can do a lot to one's spirit, including making you feel valueless, I came to experience. But when you are forced to live in the uncomfortable, crazy things can happen. And thanks to my daughter, I was able to see the beauty in it.

Some clichés should be sunsetted, but this one continues to ring true —what is one man's trash is another man's treasure. Craft store employees can't stand all the junk that piles up on the floor, but for my daughter, the junk became her hidden lifelines, meant to be signs of love to give to another.

My purpose was carved in stone the day I was born, albeit a stone I hadn't had the chance to see quite yet. Your purpose has been carved too, yet it may take overturning a lot of stones before you find the one always meant for you.

You will likely go through lots of trash cleanouts—whether you are calling the dumpster company to send you a crate to fill or others are tossing you in their proverbial ones. But don't let this trash talk get you down. The world can try to take you out like a load of rubbish, but to God you are like the fallen flower petals, beautiful hidden treasures meant to make a difference in the life of another.

Waste is all around us, but your purpose is not meant to be wasted.
Don't waste time, for it's the most precious gift ever gifted to us.
Don't waste talents, for we all have strengths we'll uncover one day.
Don't waste energy on efforts that suck you dry.
Don't waste life on earthly success; you're called to do more, be more.

God is sifting through the trash bins and finding the hidden gems in us all. He is taking out our crumpled pieces of paper, straightening the edges and writing a new and more beautiful story on the pages.

He has a purpose for you, and he plans to use your gifts—currently seen or deeply hidden—to fulfill the mission he has crafted just for you. All you have to do is believe he is working in your life, for to him, all our world's trash—our world's fallen flowers—are his beautiful treasures.

The Change

In the beginning, I, too, would dodge connection. When I would find myself in precarious circumstances, I would look at my phone, rustle through my purse or turn up the music; anything to not have to acknowledge the person standing on the side of the road looking at me.

If I don't see them, maybe they don't see me either.
Please let the light change fast so I can pass by the passerby.
Someone else will stop and help, right?! Not my problem.

I'm not alone in uttering those thoughts as my car approaches a stoplight where a homeless person is perched, trading in their dignity for a cardboard sign.

The moments are long during those uncomfortable times when it's just me and the person who is asking for help and I am dodging it. That is until things changed; until I changed.

I don't know when it happened, but once it did, it was massive. My eyes had been opened in a way I couldn't recover from. I could no longer go through the motions without seeing what otherwise I had overlooked. Dodging was no longer the answer. I needed to do something.

AFTER BEING IMPACTED BY THE CORPORATE LAYOFF, MY CAREER TOOK A PIVOT.

All I needed was packaged in a bag I carried from coffee shop to coffee shop where I worked with conversations and espresso machines as background noise. I had become a professional nomad, moving where the next business meeting took me.

Most times, I was stationed at a Starbucks where I had become a permanent fixture, much like the large oak trees that offered shade for those who conducted business on the patio. The baristas knew me, and often gifted me new caffeine concoctions to test.

But this day I was at a new stop in a different part of town, and I wasn't prepared for the limited seating the coffee shop offered. The tables were small, meant for a convo for two, outside of one large, circular table that would have made for the best Thanksgiving discussion while munching on green-bean casserole and rolls.

The table was inviting and made me smile the moment I took my first whiff of coffee beans roasting, but something was terribly off. The other tables were jam-packed. People were opting to stand to wait for their orders or continue a conversation.

While at least six or so chairs eagerly awaited a connection, no one sat at the table or even looked its way. It was as if you'd contract the plague if your gaze floated in its direction. I was baffled, but my work was calling, and I needed a seat. So, to the table I went, making myself at home. As I pulled out my notebook and my laptop from its cloth sleeve, I noticed something I had previously overlooked.

Two people were sitting at the table whispering, and upon a closer look, it was apparent that the fast-paced lifestyles around them didn't align with theirs one bit. They weren't looking for the next moment, hoping to catch it. Instead, they were grateful for the warmth this moment offered them from the chilly temperatures just outside the windows where they likely lived most of the time.

Their disheveled hair and layered clothing confirmed what my intuition began piecing together. Their lack of a computer, a phone or, quite frankly, anything, felt off in a place where work was happening all around them. Instead of vying for the newest iPhone, they were just looking for warmth and possibly some food to fill their grumbling tummies.

When you have nothing, every little thing is something not overlooked and never taken for granted.

I opened my computer to appear to work but found my eyes drawn more to their conversation. I tuned out the coffee shop hums and tuned into their moment on the other side of the table that the rest of the community was trying everything to avoid. They discussed where they could get a warm meal at a church down the street and about others who were likely a part of their homeless camp.

THEIR WORRIES WERE DIFFERENT FROM MINE.

I had a home and a credit card I could swipe if my stomach got out of control. They only owned what they could carry, and it was less than what I had stashed in my van. Their next meal was their priority; my next client was mine. We walked the same road, but our paths were completely different.

As I gazed into their world, they took notice. When everyone tries their hardest not to see you then someone finally does, you feel the gaze. I smiled. They returned the gesture, and then the lady stood to continue on her path for the day to the church to get lunch. The man, however, stayed for a few extra moments, and it was time for me to open the door to a conversation.

I don't remember how we began our discussion or how it ended, but we laughed together as we talked about the mundane. It was a brief moment we shared, and we both left smiling as he waved bye to catch up with his friend to find lunch.

The moment he left the coffee shop, the table became prime real estate for those waiting to snatch it up. What began as a lone island of opportunities in the middle of everyone's business became wanted the moment the unwanted left. I was frustrated with things in this world that seem too big for me to fix and disappointed that I didn't offer to buy this man and his friend a meal, a coffee even. I was no better than anyone else in the room.

Maybe I saw them, but I didn't meet their needs when I knew I could have. Thank heavens I had another opportunity.

THERE WAS A DIFFERENT PEP TO HIS STEP WHEN HE REENTERED STARBUCKS.

I'm confident it wasn't the caffeine from coffee behind it because he hadn't been able to afford any when I first saw him. His eyes locked on mine, and every step he took was with purpose. He was on a mission, and I was his mission.

The table had become populated since his previous exit, but there was a lone chair available next to me, and he gently pulled it away from the table to offer himself a place to rest and a place for conversation to begin again. The tedious work I was doing in cyberspace felt pointless compared to the work I was being called to do in that space. I closed my laptop and pivoted to look him directly in the eyes. He deserved to be seen this time, and I was ready for it.

Before our conversation began, I decided it was time to do what I should have done earlier. I wanted to offer to buy him something warm to take off the chill from the day.

But before I opened my mouth, he pulled out a handful of bills and asked if he could buy *me* a cup of coffee.

This gal has no poker face, so I can only imagine what was plastered on mine at that moment. Bewilderment maybe. Confusion, I'm sure. Humility, however, was behind all of it. I had begun to pull out a card, which to him was meaningless. Instead, he was not just willing but insistent upon spending the handful of bills he had to his name to buy me something. Even after I told him I wasn't a coffee drinker, he persisted, sharing it was a way he wanted to thank me for taking a moment to talk to him.

THAT DAY BECAME THE DAY I CHANGED HOW I *SEE* OTHERS.

Homelessness is a cause my family cares about, and together we purchase items for bags that we carry in our van to gift to someone who appears to need a pick-me-up from the harsh realities of street life. These kits have become a way for us to see people that many overlook, and I too once did. They are a small way we let others know we care.

Several years later, we were on an offramp about to leave the fast-paced interstate and enter one of the two country roads that would lead us home. Standing on the side of the pavement was a man and a dog, both of which our family had noticed before. We had just made it through some frigid temperatures, and we worried that the two needed a bit more than our bags had to offer, so I drove to a drive-through to gather some chicken strips while my husband ran into a country store to get a dog bone.

As we pulled back up to the place this man and his best friend stood, we waved our arms to get his attention. He had obviously become accustomed to not being the recipient of waves because he looked over his shoulder, confident we were waving to someone behind him. There wasn't anyone else; he was who we were excited to see.

We remembered his name: Mr. Keith. And his dog was Miley. He had told us the first time we gave him a kit we had on hand. We rolled down our window and welcomed the two over to the van where a warm basket of chicken tenders, salty french fries and a plastic reusable bag filled to the brim with toiletries, a blanket and snacks awaited. Mr. Keith smiled from ear to ear, and Miley began doing tricks, her tail wag constantly making a thud noise against the van in excitement.

As Mr. Keith sat down his gifts, grateful for the items within, a twenty-minute conversation ensued where he shared with us more about his life. We learned of the truck he had turned into his home. He ripped in half a chicken tender, scarfing one and using the other to show the amazing talents of his sweet girl. He shared what got him to this place and what he had left behind. I did little talking actually, but a lot of listening happened.

Mr. Keith was kind. He was grateful. He constantly imparted wisdom to my children, encouraging them to make decisions that would be fruitful and create a life easier than his.

It felt like we had known each other for decades. When I did speak, I asked him about our homeless bags, hoping to get some insights from him on the little effort we could do to make a difference in the lives of others. Did we have the right items included? What were we missing?

Mr. Keith looked at the bag from the outside, analyzing each item, and once he had, his gaze met mine and he shared something I'll always cherish.

"I don't know what else you should include. I'll think about it and let you know next time. But to be honest, the time you all have taken to talk to me—to *see* me—that is more valuable than anything this bag could ever hold."

SOME SEEDS REQUIRE DIRT FOR GROWTH.

The soil offers a plentiful amount, awaiting the chance to turn a possibility into an opportunity. Other seeds find the perfect conditions for growth in places many overlook.

A single chair, offered to someone who needs it most.
A cup of coffee, provided by someone who gave all he owned for it.
A conversation, with less talking and more listening.
A moment of time where someone else feels seen in a world that so many prefer to overlook.

Would you give all you have for one person to see you? Would you pass up physical warmth for a deeper soul-filled warmth? What we think we need to do may not be what is actually required. Change isn't only aligned with the clanking of coins; it can be found in a seed planted in the heart of another. The only conditions for that seed to grow is a healthy dose of love and a moment of one's time.

That type of change doesn't change wallets; it changes people.

The Volunteers

I came home from the annual plant sales with more tomato plants than my arms could carry in one trip. The trunk of our SUV had the grounding aroma of dirt and the remnants of it to prove it. At that time, our garden could have handled six tomato plants, eight if we pushed it. But I had purchased eighteen tomato starters, which was at least ten too many.

Each starter pack came with six plants, and I hadn't connected the dots that the three tomato plant varieties I selected meant we had six of each to add to our garden. We can make space, was the only solution I offered Cory. He shook his head and surrendered to the fact that I wasn't going to let a single one of them go.

Tighter than the experts would have preferred, we got each plant into its forever place. Like a cramped elevator experience, they smiled but wished they would have waited for the next person to pick them up, especially when the volunteers showed up.

In the gardening world, volunteers aren't like Katniss in the *Hunger Games*, volunteering to take someone's place. Instead, they are the volunteers that don't take no for an answer, opting to join the party even though they are uninvited.

WIGGLED THROUGHOUT THE EIGHTEEN TOMATO PLANTS WE PURPOSEFULLY PLANTED WERE EIGHTEEN MORE THAT, AGAINST ANY AND ALL ODDS, DECIDED TO GROW ANYWAY.

At the end of the garden season the year prior, we had done what we did every year. After picking everything we could before the bugs got to them, we would rake all the leftovers into the middle of the soil. Tomato stalks, cucumber vines and rotten leftovers created a pile and left a stench that needed to be burned, so that we did. For days the embers would crackle, and slowly our garden cleared.

We thought we were cleaning up the space.
Really, we were just planting more.

The rotten fruit had busted, which was where the foul smell protruded from. The flesh from the juicy tomatoes was no longer desirable for anything, but the seeds were still well protected and ready for action. Though the tomatoes and all else went up in flames, the seeds didn't perish. Instead, they planted under the soil, awaiting for the right conditions to germinate.

Some seeds didn't make it, but eighteen held strong and began emerging through the soil next to the intentionally planted starters.

I had noticed them when I went out to pick weeds so we could lay down recycled newspaper topped with hay as a barrier. I rubbed the leaves of the plants that looked all too familiar so I could release their fragrance and confirm my suspicions. They were, indeed, tomatoes.

I yelled for Cory so he could celebrate the unexpected news alongside me, but he wasn't quite as giddy as I was. "There is no more room for them, Steph," he unwaveringly stated. "They have to go." He saw how tightly planted the others were and was fearful we'd lose all if we kept the volunteers.

I, on the other hand, saw the situation from a much different perspective. "There is no way they are leaving," I said, as I stood up for them. "Look at what they went through to get where they are. We are in no place to stifle that growth."

I couldn't weed them out alongside the other weeds I was excavating that evening. In my core it didn't feel right. These plants had once been forgotten. They had survived through fire and manure. They had lain dormant. They were patient and persistent. I couldn't take away their growth for the sake of the others. Against Cory's recommendations, I took the wetted newspaper and created weed barriers around each, welcoming them into the garden too.

That year, our planting lines weren't straight, but our harvest was incredible. The tomato plants proved to be the most resilient, cherry tomatoes. My grandma showed me the volunteer cherry tomato plants she had peeking out from under her deck's lattice. She had never planted them, but the wind or a bird must have relocated the seeds because each year she could get more cherry tomatoes than one could ever eat alone from her plant.

Much like me, Grandma saw the volunteers as welcomed friends to her yard.

I learned water-bath canning that year, and made enough salsa to fill our bellies for several years following. When I grew tired of making salsa, I uncovered a deliciously simple pasta sauce recipe to make from cherry tomatoes, which has now become my family's favorite to use on noodles or with pizza crust. Friends begged for jars of our canned love, and we happily shared the harvest of the volunteers, which produced more fruit than the plants we originally had planted.

YEARS LATER, WHILE PREPPING FOR DINNER ONE EVENING, MY DAUGHTER ASKED IF SHE COULD HELP.

I'd always been reluctant to have my kids do anything more than set the table for fear of getting hurt. Cutting knives scared me because when I was a teen, one became lodged in my hand while I attempted to help my mom cut bread for dinner. My children weren't me, I told myself on repeat after obliging to her requested interest.

We had just begun to try a meal subscription box to ensure we were getting a variety of healthy options for dinner, so everything was pre-packaged, taking away unnecessary time sorting and meal planning. The menu that night consisted of spaghetti with a homemade tomato-basil sauce, and a cup of cherry tomatoes needed slicing. Lyndi selected the knife from our cutlery block and carefully brought it to the cutting board, determined to take the slicing off my list so I could work on the recipe's next step.

"You can trust me, Momma," she assured me. "Show me how to do it, and I'll be careful. I promise."

I picked up one tomato and walked her through the steps on how to slice it in half without slicing her hand in the process. She proceeded to delicately replicate my instruction. As I prepped the skillet and boiled water for the noodles, I smiled thinking about the beautiful pairing of two volunteers.

The cherry tomatoes volunteered growth to bear us more fruit. Lyndi volunteered time to reverently prepare the harvest.

While these tomatoes weren't from our garden, they were from someone's, and I suspected they may have been volunteers as well. Cherry tomatoes are just pesky like that, never taking no for an answer. Lyndi, too, was persistent in her request to help. She doesn't like the word no either.

One plant, one flower, one cherry tomato rotten piece of fruit has the power to pollinate. One person, one hand, one request, one opportunity has the power to feed many.

Even the overlooked, the burned, the raked or the forgotten can leave a legacy and plant hope in the hearts of others.

As with all things, your power to pollinate comes down to choice. Will you fight through barriers to stand up for what you know is right? Will you not take no for an answer, helping someone even if they give you an out to walk away? Will you volunteer to serve when you'd rather be the one served to? You hold the pollen, but it's your charge to share the gifts you have so others can be a part of your fruits harvest.

The Verb

The day I got the news, I was immediately relieved and instantaneously filled with worry. My heart wasn't in it the same way, and it was time to pivot, but I was comfortable, and change is… well, not. I needed to move on, and being laid off was the shove I needed.

I was excited about what would be on the horizon.
But I was terrified of how my family would be impacted.

The news came in November, during the month of gratitude and my favorite holiday, Thanksgiving. It butted close to December, the month where many families rack up credit card debt to offer their children a momentary happiness from things advertisers tell them they need.

Lucky for us, two of our three kids also have birthdays in December, so imagine an already hectic month turned upside down in worry and bills.

Outside of the lingering concern for how to pivot to my husband's health insurance when I was the primary provider and how to navigate unemployment, my kids were little, and the worries would have been too much for them to carry. If I was being honest with myself, they were too much for me to carry as well. I would wake up in the stillness of the night to a heavy wave of anxiety and concerns.

Would my severance be depleted over the holidays if we gave our kids the Christmas we wanted to give them but one that our accounts may not be able to sustain? How could we ensure our kids would experience the joy of the holidays when I was having a hard time finding joy myself? And their birthdays were special, but how could we not disappoint them since we couldn't give them what they'd become accustomed to receiving?

THAT'S WHEN IT HIT ME LIKE A FREIGHT TRAIN GOING A HUNDRED MILES PER MINUTE.

The force robbed me of my breath, and in its place left a kernel of an idea which would unexpectedly become the norm for our family during the holidays.

If we couldn't afford the things, maybe we shouldn't buy them.
If we didn't buy the things, what could we do instead?

Later someone shared a charge that I have embraced as my own life motto and one you are welcome to cherish as well.

Collect verbs not nouns.

Things break. They go out of style quickly. While fads come and go, they are not taken seriously, for everyone knows they will be a faded memory left for yearbook laughs in years to come.

But what doesn't abide by these rules are verbs, and they are beautiful complements to experiences. We don't remember what we wore when we learned how to walk, but we are grateful for it because it gave us the starting point to run. The look in my daughter's eyes the moment she learned to ride a bike is more valuable than the bike she received as a Christmas gift from her grandma, I'm sure, and will outlive the metal that one day will rust from being forgotten on the driveway during a rainstorm.

Experiences become etched in our minds as they are the basis of memories. And that year, we decided to give up the things and choose memories instead.

MY HUSBAND AND I HAD A POWWOW TO DETERMINE HOW TO CREATE A MEANINGFUL EXPERIENCE FOR OUR OLDER TWO CHILDREN WHO HAD BIRTHDAYS IN DECEMBER.

The outcome was a short list of two ideas and the names of two people, each holding the keys to a birthday surprise day. Cory's uncle, a groundskeeper for the local zoo, and an uncle of my cousin, who worked at the local airport, hadn't a clue that their willingness to say yes to offering up a little of their time would be the beginning of the annual birthday surprise experience tradition.

That first year, Cory's uncle unexpectedly set the bar high. We knew he worked at the zoo and asked if he would be willing to give our daughter, Lyndi, an experience around the grounds, possibly high-lighting his favorite animals along the way. Instead, he met us at the gate with a plush polar bear hidden in the depths of a Louisville Zoo branded gift bag and a surprise behind-the-scenes experience with the veterinarian who cares for the lone polar bear that roams its cage. In fact, Lyndi got to feed her and the seals too.

And Eli's birthday was soaring, literally. Unbeknownst to Cory and me, my long-distant relative worked in the airport's air traffic control directing planes. We not only got a tour of the space, but Eli's wonder was magnified as the building shook each time a plane came in for a safe landing.

The verbs we collected that year were worth more than any noun we couldn't have afforded anyway.

The following year, we picked a theme to center our birthday experiences around and landed on career paths. Our oldest wanted to be a superhero in his young age, so we scheduled time with our local law enforcement and firefighters for a special experience just for him. And Lyndi's day was easy to create because she wanted to be a princess. A friend of ours offered her the chance to ride a horse (because princesses must be comfortable doing so, of course) and we took a tour of a local castle not too far from our home.

While each year's birthday surprises become more and more difficult to create, the following year's idea was easily planted when I reached out to our favorite florist to inquire about her offering up her floral skills for our sweet Lyndi who had an affinity to flowers.

YEARS PRIOR, I REMEMBERED STEPPING FOOT INTO HER PREVIOUS FLOWER SHOP LOCATED ON A STREET THAT SEEMED LIKE IT WAS LIFTED OUT OF A HALLMARK MOVIE.

Happy storefronts in a downtown of a small city outside our hometown offered the chance for visitors to watch cinnamon candies being made and a chance to taste their spicy delights. One of my dad's favorite dives had a place where we would enjoy caponata, an Italian version of salsa. And the most glorious flower shop, a living, breathing testament to growth as seen through its floor-to-ceiling windows. Just looking in would make my day feel lighter.

My husband and I met the florist when we were planning our wedding. Our budget was tight, and this florist was determined to offer our wedding the floral beauty it we wanted at the price point we could muster up.

"Flowers shouldn't be the reason to go over budget," she once told me. "We can get creative, and they can enhance the day instead." And that is what she did.

Her artistic location is where I fell in love with green cymbidium orchids and was introduced to my favorite plant of all, the pilea. I bought my first and only air plant from her and often found myself living vicariously through her Instagram photos, daydreaming of a place where such life thrived around me daily. If we had lived closer, I'm sure I would have attempted to coax her into offering me a weekend side job just so I, too, could learn from her.

When I asked Carolyn, our forever favorite florist, if she would be up for being part of Lyndi's birthday surprise, she said yes as quickly as I asked.

Carolyn had seen Cory and I get married. She had created bouquets for our anniversaries too. She had been a part of any floral need we had and also put her loving touch on meaningful florals we would send as condolences for loss as well.

In my opinion, we all need a hairdresser, a cake designer and a florist on speed dial. And I'm grateful Carolyn is ours.

A part of birthday celebrations is the surprise element. Our kids know clearly they can't ask to add something to the surprise day, and knowledge of the day's offerings drips to them in a steady pace like the melting of ice cream over a cone in the summer's heat.

Walking into the floral shop was a full-on surprise for our little girl, and boy was she delighted.

AWAITING HER THAT DAY WAS A SURPRISE CUPCAKE SEATED BEAUTIFULLY NEXT TO THREE VASES FOR LYNDI TO CHOOSE FROM.

Carolyn, who knows our family well, had a cat mug as one of the options, and of course, it was what Lyndi chose to fill with her floral picks. Later, that mug would become one of my favorites to drink hot tea from in the mornings. Cory and I watched as Carolyn, methodically and with patience, shared her craft with our little girl.

Carolyn started with the foam core meant to offer stability and consistent water droplets to the flowers Lyndi would select. The foam is overlooked by many, but it's pivotal to the longevity of the cuts.

Next, Carolyn brought out a variety of flower selections for Lyndi and offered a story for each. Lyndi got to touch the white baby's breath and purple floral fillers. She got to inhale the fragrance of roses and lilies and learn about the uniqueness of each. Carolyn guided her to understanding color pairings and which flowers were the best of friends in arrangements. She introduced us to flowers that appeared to be imported from another world altogether, and left us all more knowledgeable about the often overlooked precision of floral arrangements.

As Lyndi pruned and clipped, I meandered the floral shop like a kid in a candy store. The flowers were abundant, and I wished I could bottle up the fragrance to become my daily perfume.

The shop had a few rooms, each with a theme and florals in alignment, and I found myself drawn to the room filled to the brim with every shade of green known to mankind. Succulents and vining greenery filled every open space on the tables within, and the room had an earthy vibe, complete with soil that I dug my fingers deep into.

It was then that I set eyes on her for the first time. The plant was out of this world, literally. I had never seen leaves that looked like UFO miniatures, and she had more legs than a family of spiders. But she was beautiful in her oddity, so I picked her up and asked Carolyn about her. The pilea plant was new to our area, I soon discovered. And Carolyn was one of the few who had one available to purchase.

Before I even learned more about the plant, I already knew she would become a staple in my home. But once Carolyn invited me to uncover what was under the loud and proud circular abundance of leaves, I was sold.

EVERY PLANT SEEKS WAYS TO CONTINUE ITS LIFELINE.

Some do so through flowers that attract pollinators to help with pollination. Others, like the aloe plant, can easily generate new roots once a leaf falls off, and like a parent dropping their kids off at college, the plant gets new footing and attempts to flourish. But the pilea is a bit different. Underneath the mother plant were tiny babies stemming from her roots. Carolyn explained that this plant propagates from its roots, and because of its ability to be easily separated, which encourages more babies to grow, it was also known as the friendship plant.

As we packed up the beautiful floral arrangement Lyndi learned to make, I also snagged that beautiful pilea, making it a staple in our home. That small plant we bought that day has grown to create more than a dozen babies, some of which we gifted or even sold to others, but many of which are placed throughout our home.

Every time I look at one, I am reminded of the power of roots, so much so that this plant is living proof that the only way to grow forward is to pull strength from the past. The present and the past are interconnected, this plant believes. New life is possibly because previous life existed, and forever this plant will continue to be a living testament to that.

But I'm also reminded of the power of verbs. My kids never ask for gifts from Cory and me, possibly because their grandparents offer them plenty. But I like to think it's because the experiences are even more enjoyable to them than a new video game or a toy destined to break or get lost.

What began as a need to offer a bit of joy during a time of immense worry and change became a sought-after and looked-forward-to tradition we all hold near and dear.

I FEEL A CONNECTION TO THE PILEA, I GUESS.

My hope is that the foundation I get to be a part of laying with my kids becomes a way in which they view the world. Every verb they collect is one they can offer. An experience offers a moment of being seen for who another truly is, and that's a gift. It's rooted in something more than the mighty dollar; it's rooted in the spirit of connection.

Sometimes you get the chance to offer the conditions for a verb to be created, like Cory and I do annually for our kids' birthdays.

Sometimes you get the chance to be the verb, like those over the years who we've asked to play a meaningful role in these celebrations by sharing a part of their passion with us.

Sometimes you get to experience what a verb really is—a living, breathing reminder of life at its core and our charge to propagate life in others.

The Stargazer

I am a practical gal, wanting little but appreciating much. I have little patience for frivolous spending and accumulating things that only collect dust. I'd rather save up for a meaningful item that is a solution to a problem I've uncovered than squander my savings on a want that will likely fade as most fads do.

I realize most people aren't like me. My husband included.
That's what makes the world tick beautifully.

WHEN CORY AND I BEGAN DATING, I MADE IT CRYSTAL CLEAR MY THOUGHTS AROUND GIFTS, HOLIDAYS AND SUCH.

Time together was my love language, not gifts of any shape or size. Walking by a case of jewelry makes me nauseated. When asked what I want for my birthday, I cringe. Likely an underlying issue of self-independence exists, but most significant others would breathe a sigh of relief knowing that their wallet will remain intact in our relationship.

Not Cory. His love language is different. It's filled to the brim with surprises and unexpected moments of celebration and love. It's beau-

tiful to be paired with the yin to your yang. His need to show gratitude pulls out in me the reminder that just because I don't need a
Valentine's Day card, he needs to gift me one. And I will forever
cherish them.

Early in our courtship, however, he did convert me to be not just a
lover of flowers but a lover of receiving them. Prior to Cory, I was
saddened when I saw fresh flowers cut from their roots only to offer a
momentary delight in someone's home.

But being on the receipt of it, I've come to love the simple and
beautiful gift for what it really is, an offering of life, of hope and
of love.

Cory has tested different flower varieties to see what I love most.
Instead of asking and getting my ho-hum answer of "I don't know and
not sure I care," he took a different approach. Each time he brought
me a bouquet, he would step back and watch my expressions. Did my
eyes glisten? Did I squeal with delight? Over time, he uncovered my
unexpected favorite: stargazer lilies. I hadn't even known they existed
before him, but now I can't imagine my life without them.

LILIES ARE LARGE AND IN CHARGE.

If you are a pro, like Cory, at picking the best bouquet, you will pick
the lilies with little to no blooms, knowing good and well to count the
number of tightly bound buds and equating it with the number of
days this bouquet would delight. Slowly, over time and with proper
water, each lily will bless the home with its presence. Striped on the
inside of each petal is a magenta smear, as if the lily attempted to put
on her own lipstick and failed miserably. It's intense and beautiful.
And she is proud of her beauty.

The color isn't the only part of the flower that I enjoy. In fact, my favorite is her aroma. While offering your eyes a guilty pleasure, the flower wants to also give your nose a gift as well. The fragrance of a lily is deep, one you can't escape from as it wants to ensure you know that it's there, waiting, for you.

After a year of homeschool teaching and selecting life science as our topic of choice, I know far too much about plants, so much so that I could actually ace a Jeopardy game on it if the opportunity arose.

The color of a flower is enticing, as is the aroma, with the intention of drawing in pollinators to fulfill a plant's true purpose of passing on its legacy.

Bees, hummingbirds and others find flowers as joyous as we do, and when they come to visit, they are bathed in pollen with the flower's hopes of taking it to the right place at the right time.

If you know stargazer lilies, you also know of their pollen. Proudly found on the tips of the flower's stamen, this powdery substance is genius for the natural world, and yet it easily stains fabric and fingers too. At first sight, I've discovered the trick for snatching that pollen before it snatches me, allowing elongated joy by watching the flowers bloom for days upon end.

I love stargazers.
My mom came to love them.
And my grandma discovered her affinity for their beauty as well.

Poor Cory became accustomed to buying three dozen stargazer lilies each time to ensure that three generations of women felt loved, were seen and enjoyed a beauty that was a mirror of the beauty he saw in us. When Cory married me, he really married all of us in the process without his knowing. But he never pushed back, seeing how his love language made each of us so happy.

I REMEMBER THE DAY I WAS TOLD THE NEWS OF MY GRANDMA'S CONDITION.

A feeling began in the pit of my stomach that quickly traveled to my throat and became lodged there for days after hearing the words: Grandma. Has. Cancer. *No, please God tell me it's not true.*

I would plead with our Maker in the hopes that he would spare someone who was a walking testament to his love. I know he listened; but the outcome wasn't what I desired.

Grandma's diagnosis came fast and with a vengeance. In the beginning, there was hope that surgery to remove a part of her lung would help. She had energy then and was willing to give it a go. I realize now that her will was really our will. She knew where she was going, but she knew we weren't ready. Are we ever? I've come to realize the answer is probably not.

I packed up my laptop and pivoted my office to her ICU hospital room as soon as they would let me in after surgery. As I was punching away at the keyboard, I heard a little whisper with a stern message. "Why are you here, Steph? You're supposed to be at work." She knew the day of the week and my workload. I hadn't told her I was coming, but there was nowhere else I wanted to be. It was important to me that she knew, from the moment she woke up on the other side of surgery, that she wasn't alone.

There I sat with two messages to share: "Grandma, I brought work here, but they wouldn't let me bring in the stargazers. The nurses say its aroma is too strong for the ICU."

When she was moved to the rehabilitation center, we bought her new stargazers, only to find that, yet again, our family's favorite flower was boycotted for its bold scent. All was well because that meant she would get to enjoy them in the comfort of her home.

GRANDMA CAME HOME, BUT SHE LEFT A PIECE OF HER BEHIND.

Her hair fell like the lily petals predictably do once their purpose is complete. Her energy wilted, and no bribing with her favorite foods could encourage her to eat because her taste buds just weren't the same. Her spirit remained strong, but the flesh became weak. She gave and gave and gave some more until there was no more to give. Her days were numbered.

Surrounded by her cherished girls, she rested in her bed those last few days in a home filled to the brim with the plants she loved and the people she constantly fertilized. Her voice was robbed of her, but like her greenery, words weren't always needed to communicate. We knew what she was saying without saying a word.

We filled the space with the words we hoped she could hear. For all the years she watered us, it was our turn to water her.

The night had come fast, and I knew the coming days were going to be hard, so I gripped Grandma's hand tight and told her I'd see her the day following. With heavy feet and a heavy heart, I walked out of her apartment to head home for what little sleep I could pull together. Ten minutes later, the phone rang, and without answering I already knew. Again, words weren't needed. I heard the news in the sniffles and through the tears.

I turned the car around and headed back to Grandma's to be with her body until I couldn't anymore. I wanted to hold on to fleeting moments for a lifetime. As I closed the door to my car and prepared to open the door to her complex, I looked up just in time to see something I've never experienced before then and haven't seen since. A shooting star.

GRANDMA WAS BOTH SAFE IN HER HEAVENLY HOME AND YET, FOREVER WITH ME.

A star in the night sky, I can find her as I gaze up to the heavens. A ray of hope in the darkness, she may have left this world, but she is rooted deep into my DNA.

I became numb as I meandered through the following days, but two memories remain. I hosted a feast at her funeral by cooking her favorites: vegetable lasagna, garlic bread and angel lush cake.

And the funeral home was filled to the brim with the aroma of stargazer lilies, her favorite.

A week or so after her passing, I had a radio interview to conduct for work. I had made friends with a radio DJ of a local gospel music channel, and monthly I would go on air to deliver a public service announcement message of cancer prevention. This interview was poignant as I had lost one of my favorite people to a cause I was desperately fighting to eradicate.

I walked in and attempted to put on a façade, only to remember that there's a reason I don't play poker. I don't have a good poker face. The DJ knew something was off and asked me if I was okay. I shared that I had lost my grandma and how I was heartbroken by it all. But even more, I was saddened because my one-day dream of growing a family meant that my children would live in a world where they would never meet such a meaningful person in my life. That just didn't seem fair.

He gave me a bear hug; you know the kind that for a split second allows someone else to carry the weight with you as you fall into their embrace. And afterward he put his hand to my chin to give it a rest while he told me something I'll never, ever forget.

"Stephanie," he said. "They will absolutely know her because they know you. She is a part of you and you a part of her. And they will love her because you love her."

I can look back now and know he was and is right. Grandma was one of the ultimate gardeners. She planted seeds of all kinds and watered them with precision and purpose. She tilled and cared for every seed she planted and offered the conditions for growth. And of course her favorite flower would be the same as mine... a stargazer lily. A poignant reminder that the real purpose of our lives is to leave a legacy while planting seeds and always gazing up at the heavens in the process.

Now she lives among the stars.
And I am blessed with the opportunity to be the gazer.

Emergence

L ate one evening, when the rest of the world was deep in slumber, my husband had a vision.

Instead of getting the much-needed rest our bodies desperately yearned for, that evening, after we had put our kids to bed, the two of us sat on the couch finding solace in the latest television craze. We love to binge watch intriguing shows, as it gives us a break from life and the many hats we wear and allows us to be transported into another scene with a plot very different from ours.

Deeply enthralled by the motions on the screen, it took me a moment to understand that I had unexpectedly heard something that I rarely got to hear. Silence.

No sound was a new sound in our household, and it was one I was navigating as the television screen went still. My husband had pressed pause—on the TV but not on his thoughts. And as I turned to question why he would do such a thing, stopping a show mid-action, his face told me everything. I knew he had to tell me something more important than any word some meaningless character could have spoken.

He shared a vision he had just had of me on a stage, delivering a speaking engagement about a topic that was destined to leave a lasting impact. He spoke of a theme that I had never contemplated and a platform I was terrified of failing at. He went as far as sketching out the graphic elements that accompanied my presence on the stage and left me with the charge to make it happen.

WHILE I WAS NEARING THE COMPLETION OF MY FIRST BOOK, I HADN'T A CLUE WHAT THE NEXT CHAPTER OF MY LIFE WOULD ENTAIL.

I hadn't thought about what I would be doing in the next ten minutes, much less what I would be doing in the next ten months or ten years. But I did what anyone would have done who saw the seriousness of his face—I didn't let his thoughts go to waste. I went to work.

By the end of that year, I had collaborated with a dear friend to bring the envisioned graphics he saw to life. Six very simple but very profound images sat in a folder buried deep within my computer's system waiting for their purpose, waiting for their moment. And then I received the call.

My college alma mater is seated high on top of hill, a beautiful campus in the heart of the city I was born in, raised in and have always known best. I had graduated quite some time prior to that moment but always felt something within telling me I was meant to do more, that I was supposed to go back and give to the school as it had given to me. When I received the call, it all finally made sense.

The university was looking for a speaker to engage with a selective audience on a beautiful day in spring. A group of budding women, hand-selected for their leadership potential, would join together at a banquet, the culmination of a year's effort to become true women in leadership poised to change communities and the world at large. The group was easy to support, but it was the theme that solidified my involvement.

Emergence.

Every word on that call brought to life the vision my husband had had months prior. Each graphic my friend had carefully designed was exactly what the staff member on the phone was asking for. The goal of the banquet was the goal of my life, and the moment I stood on stage engaging the audience in a topic planted within me before the committee planned the event, I knew my husband's vision had finally bloomed.

Nothing about that day happened because I was willing to be. It happened because the conditions were right and ready.

I had tried years prior to identify an opportunity for collaboration but to no avail. However it was the seed of the idea that finally took root and was given a chance. I was forced to step into the uncomfortable and break through my limiting beliefs holding tight about my value, my worth and my message for this to happen and for blooming to be possible. But I realized that day the true beauty of the moment wasn't what I brought to the table, but how I was able to pollinate others.

A SEED DOESN'T BECOME A TREE OVERNIGHT.

You can attempt to watch a plant grow, but it's much like watching paint dry: painful and uneventful. Growth comes with moments that appear stagnant, but sometimes growth doesn't only happen above the soil, but it also happens below and within. Everything is needed for thriving life in a single seed, but the conditions must be perfect for the sequence to begin. Your timing and the seed's timing aren't usually in lockstep.

If you've identified a seed of an opportunity within you, there is a path that will likely unfold before you.

It is laced with persistence and doubt, for storms are ahead and the challenges are plentiful. The first breakthrough will be hard, and it will likely come when you are on the verge of tossing the seed out altogether and giving up entirely. Don't. Instead, realize at that moment the seed wants to grow; in fact, it's designed to. Step out of its way, and let it happen by offering it the conditions to thrive.

Nourish it well, and love on it daily. Believe in its possibilities and surround yourself with others who do too. Give it sun and water. And turn it ever so slightly to strengthen its stalk. Don't hide it from storms, but allow it to be strengthened by them. Care for its roots as for its blooms, for the past and future both matter. Celebrate its milestones, for each breakthrough is meaningful and likely difficult. And when it's completed its purpose, smile knowing you were given the chance to be a part of it as it's now a part of you too.

People often ask me if I am a rainbow-and-butterflies kind of gal, someone who is always optimistic, and let me tell you, I am one but for a whole different reason. I love rainbows because it's a wonderful reminder that going through the rain doesn't mean something beautiful isn't on the other side. I love butterflies, but it's because the caterpillar had to make the decision to go through change and emerge more beautiful than before. And I love flowers, but not just when they bloom but for the emergence they go through to get there and the perseverance they go through to pollinate others.

Take a moment to open the blinds and feel the sun's rays beam on your face and into your soul. Before you close this book, take a deep breath, inhaling this moment and the beautiful life you've been gifted. Before you go back to the busyness of what I can only expect is a chaotic life, close your eyes and seek an openness to what the world is waiting to give you.

As the sun warms your spirit and the air fills your lungs, listen to the seed calling within you, begging for the conditions to grow so it can change the life of another in the process.

It's begging to emerge.
Will you let it?

Life's Gardening Tips

We're not that different from a plant. We both grow and need the conditions to do so. We both are charged with growing life. We both need air and water to survive. We both communicate, although one is a bit louder than the other. Throughout the pages, you've gleaned wisdom from what nature has taught me, and I pray it will continue to help you grow even more.

But your learning isn't complete now that the book is.
Instead, you've just begun.

As you continue your own personal growth, let me leave you with some powerful takeaways to consider.

Everything a seed needs is found within it.

And everything you need to grow is within you too. You may need to break free from your outer casing a bit, but trust in the fact that you have the tools (and know where to find them if needed) so be the you that you are called to be. All the seed needs to begin growth is action. Find the courage to be brave and take it.

Your roots ground you.

Your past doesn't have to define you, but it can refine you, creating a foundation for you to weather future storms. Your roots are adaptable, however, and able to break free from their restricted confines so that you can become anchored in your truth. They offer you support, and they are powerful. Use their power for good.

You can and will break through.

While knee-deep in manure, never forget that your darkest of days may be fertilizing your soil for the sunrise ahead. For breakthroughs to happen, you need more than what can be seen. You need hardships, offering fertilizer for growth. You need community, becoming rocks for stabilization. If a tiny seed can experience a breakthrough, anything is possible for you.

Growth requires patience.

Listen to your body like I listen to plants. It tells you what it needs to grow if you create space to hear it. Take time to pull the weeds and rehydrate when you are parched. You can't give to others if you don't have anything left of you to give. Use the tools you have, including your breath, to embrace the moment. Growth is the goal, but the journey to it is just as important.

Never seek to bloom too soon.

Blooming may feel like a pinnacle for our own success, but its true purpose isn't to get but to give. A flower's bloom attracts pollinators. Our blooms should become beacons for others, so that they, too, can show their true colors and fulfill their passions and purpose. Your single bloom can and will change lives if you let it.

Our life's goal should be pollination.

You were made to be you because the world needs you. It needs exactly who you are and who you are destined to become. You are a part of God's puzzle, and for the puzzle to become complete, he needs you and everyone around you. Every experience is a lesson; every lesson is an opportunity. What you do with it will determine if you hoard your pollen or if you share it. It's in sharing where true growth happens and where legacy is found.

Finding your seed is just the start.
Using it for the good of others is its sole purpose.

Roll Up Your Sleeves

LET'S GET IN THE WEEDS

You've read these pages and soaked in the lessons.
It's time for you to till your garden and sow.
Harvest time is coming, and you deserve to enjoy a bountiful crop.

If you are ready to emerge, make it happen. Stephanie would be honored to roll up her sleeves alongside you, your group or your organization and get in the weeds. She doesn't just plant vegetable seeds, she plants seeds of purpose everywhere she goes.

Personally or professionally, Stephanie can help you breakthrough and break free by creating the conditions for growth to thrive best. Invite her to engage with your group through:

- Engaging keynote addresses
- Experiential, hands-on workshops
- Deep-dive retreats
- And more!

To learn more about Stephanie's suite of offerings or to schedule her to come and engage with your group, visit www.StephanieFeger.com.

Acknowledgments

A tree doesn't grow alone on its own or without some help. Whether it's aware of it or not, something was before it, something came alongside it, and one day, something will come forth because of it. A single tree likely won't make it alone, without the support of others.

Much like a tree, a house plant, a flower or a vegetable starter, I haven't grown in a stark greenhouse where I was the only one enduring the humid temperatures. And I'm forever grateful that I didn't have to. In fact, so many people fertilized my soil, planted seeds of opportunity, tilled the land and have watered me daily. For each and every one of them, I'm eternally grateful.

From a young age, my mom and dad saw in me more than I ever saw in myself. As I uncovered my seeds of potential, they offered me room to stumble and learn and a helping hand to stand back up each time. Because of who they were and the people who poured into them along their journeys, they both helped me grow solid roots that have forever kept me grounded. I am forever grateful for them allowing me to reach for the sun every twist and turn I experienced and never pruning my ideas. Instead, they let them get unwieldy and brought their pruning shears to help me trim the excess when I was ready, not when they were. If I could have hand-picked two people to learn the most from, I would pick my mom and dad over and over again.

My husband, Cory, constantly waters all of my seedlings, seeing my new beginnings as exciting as I do. And, when I'm busy planting a new idea, he is nurturing the others I started, letting me know first when new growth happens. Many times, it's hard to see growth in yourself, but Cory is my constant supporter, ready to roll up his sleeves and get in the dirt with me if I ask and offer support when I feel like I'm wilting and drooping. I am grateful that not only have we been able to grow together as a pairing—one that goes together nicely like peas and carrots—we have been able to grow a family, too, and see the fruits of our hard work. The droughts filled with concern... the feast or famine feelings of worry and joy... the hardships of loss and the celebrations of triumph... he has been with me every step of the way. I see you, Cory, and I'm overjoyed.

Eli, Lyndi and Luke are my three most precious seeds. Each of them was prayed for and nurtured from the moment they came to be. While gardening may come with an almanac for guidance, parenting has no guidebook, and I'm confident I've made mishaps in my journey through it. I'm grateful for the grace they offer and the teachings each provide me daily. Sometimes, my leaves are the highest, offering them shade and respite. Other times, these three bring me water as we hold hands and soak in God's beauty around us. While I sure do love my plants, my garden and my flowers, what they may not realize is that I see each of them in all of it. And they are my most cherished seedlings. Pouring goodness into their hearts has been the greatest fruit of my labor, and I am grateful to be their gardener and their momma.

So many people have been a part of my growth, offering different nutrients into my soil, but my grandparents have, by far, taught me the importance of soil in the first place. The day my Grandma and Grandpa Schrenger bought their twenty-five-acre heaven, I began to experience God in completely different ways. From our weekend trips sleeping in the smallest trailer that I am confident was not made for five people to squish in to us having Halloween hayrides and large family kickball tournaments, this space was a respite from any worry we carried. The memories made high in the treehouse my dad built, complete with plenty of his blood, sweat and tears (literally) to those deep in the gushing overflowing creek bed will always be a part of me.

When I think of my Grandma Schrenger, who passed away in 2022, I remember the woman who could turn anything from the garden into a meal better than any chef could concoct and the woman who used this land to love her people so incredibly deeply that you felt her love miles before reaching the property. I love reminiscing with my Grandpa Schrenger about the times when Ferdinand the bull let us know that he ran the show. When he jumped the fence to fight a rogue neighboring bull that meandered onto our property, he reminded us that the fence we thought kept him in was just a formality. In fact, he chose to graze on our preferred side of the fence line, not the other way around.

My Grandma Lamaster, who I lovingly dubbed Grandma with the Candy Bowl, didn't have a farm or even a backyard for that matter. But that didn't stop her from seeing God's beauty in the greenery. In fact, much like I felt visiting the farm, my pulse rate would decrease and my heart itself would grow three times bigger when I would walk past the luscious begonias on the apartment's front steps and smelled her fried chicken in the skillet immediately when I opened the door to her complex. Time stopped when I stepped foot in her home. Minutes felt like hours when we were together gazing at her African violets, holiday cacti and philodendron. I may have said goodbye for the last time to this amazing woman in 2010, but she continues to be a teacher of mine to this day.

For every season of life has come beautiful blooming friendships. There aren't enough trees to create the pages needed to count them all. But each has played a major part in the strengthening of my own tree trunk. For the friendships that have been like the changing of leaves or the growing of limbs, thank you for being beautiful when and where I needed you and for offering me adventure when I was looking for a climb. For the friendships that offered me an embrace when life became troubling and unbearable, like a tree's bark, I appreciate the protection and comfort so I could weather any storm. For the friendships that have become a part of my root system, thank you for loving all parts of who I am and holding strong when I wanted to let the wind consume me. I'll never, ever be able to say thank you enough.

The Master Gardener, however, has been my greatest teacher. While I still have much growth to do and learning to embrace, I've come to find joy in the manure and solace in the pollination. I'm learning to offer a sway when the wind does blow, trusting that my roots are strong enough to keep me upright. God has been and always will be my source of light and nourishment. I'm grateful for his constant watering and for the reminders that rainbows are found after the showers.

We aren't much different from life right outside our window; in fact, we are extremely interconnected. And I'm eternally indebted to my garden for reminding me that a single seed, against all odds, really, truly wants to grow and will do anything possible to make it happen. If it can achieve its goal, I remain grounded in the fact that maybe I can too.

About the Author

Stephanie Feger is living proof that any city girl can become a farmer if she desires to. She happily trades nail polish for soil in her nail beds thanks to the love for the outdoors planted within her as a little girl. She feels most at peace when the fall season invites the pesky ticks into their hibernating slumber and she can hike to the bubbling creek in the deepest part of her family's farm to wade in the water. It's an author's paradise, flooding her thoughts with inspiration.

Her family of five has grown by leaps and bounds since moving to their twenty-five-acre farm in Kentucky. Redbird Farm, as they call it, is a safe haven to more than just Stephanie; her husband, Cory; and their three kiddos—Eli, Lyndi and Luke. They've accumulated a zoo of permanent residents—six cats: Baby, Timmy, Oreo, Snickers, Tom and Luna—and the sweetest dog on the planet, Zoey. In addition, each year they foster nearly a dozen helpless kittens found throughout Kentucky in need of loving homes. Want Stephanie to go down a rabbit trail of stories? Ask her about her foster favorites. (Hint: They all are!)

Stephanie is a book marketing whiz who supports authors in promoting marketable books and building budding businesses from empowering messages. As the owner of the emPower PR Group, a boutique marketing solution for nonfiction authors, she sees the seeds of possibilities within many and offers the conditions to help them bloom into beautiful, pollinating and life-giving messages destined to change lives.

Her greatest joy is watching her kids grow into the people God called them to be. Seeing their potential bloom is living proof that sometimes you are the seed, and other times you are the flower, but all the time you can reap the benefits of what you or others sow.

When she isn't helping her clients, enjoying the cathartic release of writing herself or cutting grass at turbo speeds on the riding lawn mower, Stephanie enjoys hiking in the mountains of the Red River Gorge, attempting to grow veggie starters even though she knows she will likely not succeed at hardening them, perusing the local hardware store to snatch up a weary house plant to nurse, going to the movies with her family and eating a whole bag of popcorn herself, and spending time reflecting on God's beauty in her every day.

Learn more at StephanieFeger.com.

Also by Stephanie Feger

Emergence: Living Lessons from the Soil is Stephanie Feger's fourth published book, although many more continue to marinate, awaiting their opportunity to be nurtured and shared with those who could be inspired by her messages of hope, empowerment, perseverance and impact.

Her first book, *Color Today Pretty: An Inspirational Guide to Living a Life in Perspective*, was the beginning of a new calling for her. It unexpectedly charged her to merge her love with her passion, and it continues to inspire her to always let perspective guide her way.

Her second book, *Color Today Pretty Guided Journal*, is a complement to her first, inviting readers to bring her insights into their lives in an active way, chronicling their life experience alongside the inspirational messages found within.

Stephanie's third book, *Make Your Author emPact: Sell More Books, Increase Your Reach & Achieve Your Why*, captures her unique book marketing insights to help authors ensure that those who need their books know about them and buy them.

Learn more about her books at StephanieFeger.com.

Color Today Pretty: An Inspirational Guide to Living a Life in Perspective

Through relatable and powerful true stories, Stephanie inspires you to live life more richly. Learn how to rise above disappointment or hardship, prevent monotony from clouding your ability to savor profound moments and hold onto happiness and faith no matter what.

Color Today Pretty is more than a book —it's a way of living that underscores the need for compassion, curiosity and unwavering love. Take an intimate walk with reflection and explore how true perspective changes everything—including how we love, forgive, appreciate and awaken to new possibilities.

Color Today Pretty Guided Journal

Whether you have read or are currently reading Color Today Pretty: An Inspirational Guide to Living a Life in Perspective and are seeking to bring the words off the page and into your life, this journal is designed for you. Begged for by readers of her first book, the Color Today Pretty Guided Journal parallels Stephanie's life-giving stories while offering readers the space to reflect on each.

Looking for a tool to help you, your group or your organization utilize for deeper reflection? This journal provides structure for personal and group reflection and creative elements for unique learning. Your journey toward perspective awaits! Change doesn't live in a book; it's invited into your life. The only requirement is making the choice to welcome it in.

Make Your Author emPact: Sell More Books, Increase Your Reach & Achieve Your Why

You wrote a book or are planning to. Now, how do you use it to make your author emPact? Most authors focus intensely on writing a book. But that's only part of the author process. Without marketing, a book will never fulfill its purpose. (And a book that isn't read breaks Stephanie's heart.)

Stephanie wrote *Make Your Author emPact* for writers, authors and authorpreneurs who want to make an emPact—and know marketing will make that happen—but are unsure of the next right move. Whether traditionally published, self-published or somewhere in between, Stephanie distills marketing strategies and tactics that will help any and all authors sell more books, increase their reach and achieve their why.

Made in the USA
Columbia, SC
14 April 2023

15090737R00141